Aristophanes: Frogs

The Focus Classical Library

Aristophanes
Frogs

Translated with
Introduction and Notes

Jeffrey Henderson
Boston University

Focus an imprint of
Hackett Publishing Company, Inc.
Indianapolis/Cambridge

Frogs
© 2008 Jeffrey Henderson

Previously published by Focus Publishing/R. Pullins Company

Focus an imprint of
  Hackett Publishing Company, Inc.
  P.O. Box 44937
  Indianapolis, Indiana 46244-0937

  www.hackettpublishing.com

Cover Photo: Copyright Alex Bramwell

ISBN: 978-1-58510-308-9

Contents

INTRODUCTION

Aristophanes and Old Comedy

Aristophanes of Athens, the earliest comic playwright from whom whole works survive, was judged in antiquity to be the foremost poet of Old Attic Comedy, a theatrical genre of which he was one of the last practitioners and of which his eleven surviving plays are our only complete examples. His plays are valued principally for the exuberance of their wit and fantasy, for the purity and elegance of their language, and for the light they throw on the domestic and political life of Athens in an important era of its history. Legend has it that when the Syracusan tyrant Dionysius wanted to inform himself about "the republic of the Athenians," Plato sent him the plays of Aristophanes.

Little is known about Aristophanes' life apart from his theatrical career. He was born *ca*. 447/6, the son of one Philippus of the urban deme Cydathenaeum and the tribe Pandionis, and he died probably between 386 and 380. By his twenties his hair had thinned or receded enough that his rivals could call him bald. He seems to have had land-holdings on, or some other connection with, the island of Aegina, a connection that detractors and enemies exploited early in his career in an attempt to call his Athenian citizenship into question. In the 420s he was twice prosecuted by a fellow demesman, the popular politician Cleon, for the political impropriety of two of his plays (*Babylonians* of 426 and *Knights* of 424), but neither time was he convicted. Early in the fourth century he represented his tribe in the prestigious government position of Councillor. Four comic poets of the fourth century, Araros, Philetaerus, Philippus and Nicostratus, are reputed in ancient sources to be his sons.

In his dialogue *Symposium* Plato chose Aristophanes to represent comedy, a sign that soon after his death Aristophanes was already regarded as the genre's preeminent practitioner. Plato portrays him as being at home among the social and intellectual elite of Athens. Although the historical truth of Plato's portrayal is uncertain, subsequent tradition agreed about Aristophanes' professional and literary stature, and Aristophanes' plays do generally espouse the social, moral and political sentiments of contemporary upper-class conservatives: nostalgia for the good old days of the early democracy, which defeated the Persians and built the empire; dismay at the decadence, corruption and political divisiveness of his own day; hostility toward the new breed of populist leaders who emerged after the death of the aristocratic Pericles in 429; impatience with the leadership and slow progress of the Peloponnesian War (431-404), particularly when it threatened the interests of the land-owning classes; and unhappiness about many of the artistic and intellectual trends of his own day, especially those he regarded as harming the high art of drama. There is no question that Aristophanes' comic expression of such views reflected, and to a degree shaped, community opinion, and that comedy could occasionally have a distinct social and political impact. But the fact that Aristophanes emerged politically and artistically unscathed from the war, from two oligarchic revolutions (411 and 404), and from two democratic restorations (411 and 403) suggests that on the whole his role in Athenian politics was more satirical, moral(istic) and poetical than practical; and the perennial popularity of his plays would seem to indicate that the sentiments they express were broadly shared at least among the theatrical public.

The period of Old Comedy at Athens began in 486 BC, when comedy first became part of the festival of the Greater Dionysia; by convention it ended in 388 BC, when Aristophanes produced his last play. During this period some 600 comedies were produced. We know the titles of some fifty comic poets and the titles of some 300 plays. We have eleven complete plays by Aristophanes, the first one (*Acharnians*) dating from 425, and several thousand fragments of other plays by Aristophanes and other poets, most of them only a line or so long and very few deriving from plays written before 440.

The principal occasions for the production of comedies were the Greater Dionysia, held in late March or early April, and (from 440) the Lenaea, held in late January or early February. These were national festivals honoring the wine-god Dionysus, whose cult from very early times had included mimetic features. The theatrical productions that were the highlight of the festivals were competitions in which poets, dancers, actors, producers and musicians competed for prizes that were awarded by judges at the close of the festival. The Greater Dionysia was held in the Theater of Dionysus on the south slope of the Acropolis, which in the fifth century accommodated 4,000 to 10,000 spectators, including both Athenian and foreign visitors, and by the fourth century as many as 17,000. The Lenaea, which only Athenians attended, was held elsewhere in the city (we do not know where). By the fourth century the Lenaea was held in the Theater of Dionysus also, but it is unclear when the relocation occurred.

At these festivals comedy shared the theater with tragedy and satyr-drama, genres that had been produced at the Greater Dionysia since the sixth century. The first "city" contest in tragedy is dated to 534, when the victorious actor-poet was Thespis (from whose name actors are still called thespians). But it is not certain that Thespis' contest was held at the Greater Dionysia, and in any case this festival seems to have experienced major changes after the overthrow of the tyranny and the establishment of democracy, that is, after the reforms of Cleisthenes in 508. Tragedy dramatized stories from heroic myth, emphasizing dire personal and social events that had befallen hero(in)es and their families in the distant past, and mostly in places other than Athens. By convention, the poetry and music of tragedy were highly stylized and archaic. Satyr-drama, which was composed by the same poets who wrote tragedy, had similar conventions, except that the heroic stories were treated in a humorous fashion and the chorus was composed of satyrs: mischievous followers of Dionysus who were part human and part animal.

Comedy, by contrast, had different conventions of performance (see on Production, below) and was less restricted by conventions of language, music and subject. That is probably why the composers and performers of tragedy and satyr-drama were never the same ones who composed and performed comedy. The language of comedy was basically colloquial, though it often parodies the conventions of other (particularly tragic) poetry, and was free to include indecent, even obscene material. The music and dancing, too, tended to reflect popular styles. The favorite subjects of comedy were free-form mythological burlesque; domestic situations featuring everyday character types; and political satire portraying people and events of current interest in the public life of the Athenians. Our eleven surviving comedies all fall into this last category. Mythological and domestic comedy continued to flourish after the Old Comic period, but political comedy seems to have died out: a casualty not merely of changing theatrical tastes but also of the social and political changes that followed the Athenians' loss of the Peloponnesian War, and with it their empire, in 404. To understand the significance of political comedy, we must look first at the political system of which it was an organic feature: the phase of radical democracy inaugurated by the reforms of Ephialtes in 462/1 and lasting until the end of the century.

Democracy means "rule of the demos" (sovereign people). In fifth-century Athens democracy was radical in that the sovereignty of the demos was more absolute than in any other society before or since. The demos consisted of all citizen males at least eighteen years of age. All decisions affecting the governance and welfare of the state were made by the direct and unappealable vote of the demos. The state was managed by members of the demos at least thirty years of age, who were chosen by lot from a list of eligible citizens and who held office in periods ranging from one day to one year. The only exceptions were military commanders, who were elected to one-year terms, and holders of certain ancient priesthoods, who inherited their positions. The demos determined by vote whether or not anyone holding any public position was qualified to do his job, and after completion of his term, whether he had done it satisfactorily. All military commanders, and most holders of powerful allotted offices, came from the wealthy classes, but their success depended on the good will of the demos as a whole.

One of the most important allotted offices in the democracy was that of choregus, sponsor of a chorus. Choregi were allotted from a list of men wealthy enough to hold this office, for they had to recruit and pay for the training, costuming and room and board of the chorus that would perform at one of the festivals. In the case of a comic chorus this involved 24 dancers and the musicians who would accompany them. Being choregus gave a man an opportunity to display his wealth and refinement for the benefit of the demos as a whole and to win a prize that would confer prestige on himself and his dancers. Some wealthy men therefore volunteered to be a choregus instead of waiting for their names to be drawn. On the other hand, a man who put on a cheap or otherwise unsatisfactory chorus could expect to suffer a significant loss of public prestige.

All other festival expenses, including stipends for the poet and his actors and for prizes, were undertaken by vote of the demos and paid for from public funds. A poet got a place in the festival by submitting a draft some six months in advance to the office-holder in charge of the festival. Ancient sources say that at least the choral parts of the proposed play had to be submitted. How much more was submitted we do not know. But revision up to the day of the performance was certainly possible, since many allusions in comedy refer to events occurring very shortly before the festival: most notably the death of Sophocles shortly before the performance of *Frogs* in 405.

If he got on the program, the poet would be given his stipend and assigned his actors. He and the choregus would then set about getting the performance ready for the big day, the poet acting as music master, choreographer and director, the choregus rounding up, and paying the expenses of, the best dancers he could find. While tragic poets produced three tragedies and a satyr-drama, comic poets produced only one comedy.

Thus comedy, as a theatrical spectacle, was an organic feature of Athenian democracy. But its poetic, musical and mimetic traditions were much older, deriving from forms of entertainment developed by cultivated members of the aristocratic families that had governed Attica before the democracy. One such traditional form was the komos (band of revellers), which gave comedy (*komoidia* "song of the komos") its name. A komos was made up of some solidary group (a military, religious or family group, for example), often in masks or costumes, which entertained onlookers on many kinds of festive and religious occasions.

Part of the entertainment was abuse and criticism of individuals or groups standing outside the solidarity of the komos. The victims might be among the onlookers or they might be members of a rival komos. The komos sang and danced as a group, and its leader (who was no doubt also the poet) could speak by himself to his komos, to the onlookers or to a rival komos-leader. No doubt at a very early stage the komos was a competitive entertainment by which a given group could, in artistic ways, make those claims and criticisms against rival groups which at other times they might make in more overtly political ways. The targets of komastic abuse were often the village's most powerful men and groups. Thus the tradition of the komos was useful in allowing the expression of personal and political hostilities which would otherwise have been difficult to express safely: the misbehavior of powerful individuals, disruptive but unactionable gossip, the shortcomings of citizens in groups or as a whole. Here komos served a cathartic function, as a kind of social safety valve, allowing a relatively harmless airing of tensions before they could become dangerous, and also as a means of social communication and social control, upholding generally held norms and calling attention to derelictions.

But in addition to its critical and satiric aspects, komos (like all festive activities) had an idealistic side, encouraging people to envision the community as it would be if everyone agreed on norms and lived up to them, and a utopian side as well, allowing people to imagine how wonderful life would be if reality were as human beings, especially ordinary human beings, would like it to be. In this function komos provided a time-out from the cares and burdens of everyday life.

Old Comedies were theatrical versions of komos: the band of dancers with their leader was now a comic chorus involved in a story enacted by actors on a stage. The chorus still resembled a komos in two ways: (1) as performers, it competed against rival choruses, and (2) in its dramatic identity it represented, at least initially, a distinct group or groups: in *Frogs*, for example, its members impersonated a mixed (male and female, and perhaps young and old) initiates of the Eleusinian Mysteries. The comic chorus differs from a komos in that at any given point in a play it may drop its dramatic identity, since to some degree it always represents the festival's traditional comic chorus and thus reflects the celebrating community as a whole. In a comedy's choral parabasis (self-revelation) the chorus leader often steps forward, on behalf of the poet, to advise and admonish the spectators, and between episodes the chorus often sings abusive songs about particular individuals in the audience.

The actors in the stage-area had been amalgamated with the chorus during the sixth century. Their characteristic costumes (see Production, below) and antics were depicted in vase-paintings of that period in many parts of Greece, suggesting a much older tradition of comic mimesis. As early as the Homeric period (8th and 7th centuries) we find mythological burlesque and such proto-comedy as the Thersites-episode in the second book of the *Iliad*. In this period, too, the iambic poets flourished. Named for the characteristic rhythm of their verses, which also became the characteristic rhythm of actors in Athenian drama, the iambic poets specialized in self-revelation, popular story-telling, earthy gossip, and personal enmities, often creating fictitious first-person identities and perhaps also using masks and disguise. They were credited with pioneering poetic styles invective, obscenity and colloquialism, some of them adopted by the later comic poets, including Aristophanes.

The characters on the Old Comic stage preserved many of these traditions, but like the chorus they were an adaptation to the democratic festivals, most notably in political comedy. In Aristophanes's plays, the world depicted by the plot and the characters on stage was the world of the spectators in their civic roles: as heads of families and participants in governing the democratic state. We see the demos in its various capacities; the competitors for public influence; the men who hold or seek offices; the social, intellectual and artistic celebrities. We hear formal debate on current issues, including its characteristic invective. We get a decision, complete with winners and losers, and we see the outcome. This depiction of public life was designed both to arouse laughter and to encourage reflection about people and events in ways not possible in other public contexts. Thus it was at once a distorted and an accurate depiction of public life, somewhat like a modern political cartoon.

Aristophanic comedies typically depict Athens in the grip of a terrible and intractable problem (e.g. the war, bad political leaders, an unjust jury-system, dangerous artistic or intellectual trends), which is solved in a fantastic but essentially plausible way, often by a comic hero. The characters of these heroic plays fall into two main categories, sympathetic and unsympathetic. The sympathetic ones (the hero and his/her supporters), are fictitious creations embodying ideal civic types or representing ordinary Athenians. The unsympathetic ones embody disapproved civic behavior and usually represent specific leaders or categories of leaders. The sympathetic characters advocate positions held by political or social minorities and are therefore "outsiders." But they are shown winning out against the unsympathetic ones, who represent the current status quo. Characters or chorus-members representing the demos as a whole are portrayed as initially sceptical or hostile to the sympathetic character(s), but in the end they are persuaded; those responsible for the problem are disgraced or expelled; and Athens is recalled to a sense of her true (traditional) ideals and is thus renewed. In the (thoroughly democratic) comic view, the people are never at fault for their problems, but are merely good people who have been deceived by bad leaders. Thus the comic poets tried to persuade the actual demos (the spectators) to change its mind about issues that had been decided but might be changed (e.g. the war, as in *Acharnians* and *Lysistrata*), or to discard dangerous novelties (e.g. Socratic science and rhetoric, as in *Clouds*). Aristophanes at least once succeeded: after the performance of *Frogs* in 405 he was awarded a crown by the city for the advice that was given by the chorus-leader in that play and that was subsequently adopted by the demos.

In this way, the institution of Old Comedy performed functions essential to any democracy: public airing of minority views and criticism of those holding power. Thus the Old Comic festivals were in part a ritualized protest by ordinary people against its advisers and leaders. But they were also an opportunity to articulate civic ideals: one identified the shortcomings of the status quo by holding it up against a vision of things as they ought to (or used to) be. The use of satire and criticism within a plot addressing itself to important issues of national scope was thus a democratic adaptation of such pre-democratic traditions as komos and iambic poetry. That the comic festivals were state-run and not privately organized, a partnership between the elite and the masses, is striking evidence of the openness and self-confidence of a full democracy: the demos was completely in charge, so it did not fear attacks on its celebrities or resent admonition by the poets. In particular, the Athenians were much less inclined than we are to treat their political leaders with fear and reverence: since the Athenian people were themselves the government, they tended to see their leaders more as advisors and competitors for public stature than august representatives of the state. And even comic poets enjoyed the traditional role of Greek poets and orators generally: to admonish, criticise and advise on behalf of the people. In Socrates' case, the demos seems to have taken Aristophanes' criticisms to heart, however exaggerated they may have been: as Plato reported in his *Apology*, the *Clouds'* "nonsensical" portrait of Socrates was a factor in the people's decision, twenty-four years later, to condemn him to death.

The comic poets did not, however, enjoy a complete license to say anything they pleased: were that the case they could not have expected anyone to take what they had to say seriously. Following each festival there was an assembly in which anyone who had a legal complaint could come forward. Although the Athenians recognized freedom of speech, they did not tolerate all speech. No one who spoke in public, comic poets included, could criticize the democratic constitution and the inherent rightness of the demos' rule, or say anything else that might in some way harm the democracy or compromise the integrity of the state religion. And abuse of individuals could not be slanderous. But the Athenian definition of slander differed from ours; our slander laws are designed to protect individuals, whereas the Athenian slander laws were designed to protect the institutions of the democracy: they forbade malicious and unfounded abuse of individuals if and only if the abuse might compromise a man's civic standing or eligibility to participate in the democracy, for example, accusations that would, if taken seriously, make a man ineligible to participate in public life. And so, if the criticism and abuse we find in Old Comedy often seems outrageous by our standards, it is because we differ from the fifth-century Athenians in our definition of outrageous, not because comic poets were held to no standards.

Aristophanes, for example, was twice sued by the politician Cleon, once for slandering the demos and its officers in front of visiting foreigners (in *Babylonians* of 426) and once for slandering him (in *Knights* of 424). In the first instance the demos decided not to hear the case. In the second the poet and the politician settled out of court (in *Wasps* of 422, Aristophanes subsequently boasted that he had not abided by the agreement). The demos could also enact new laws restricting comic freedoms, to protect the integrity of the military or legal systems. One of these laws was enacted in 440, when Athens went to war against her own ally Samos; another, enacted in 415, forbade mention by name in comedy of any of the men who had recently been implicated in the parody of the Eleusinian Mysteries of Demeter. Possibly the demos wanted to protect from public innuendo those who might be suspected, but might not ultimately be convicted, of this crime: as we have seen, such innuendo would fall within the legal definition of slander. And possibly the demos did not want to take the chance that a comic poet might speak sympathetically of the profaners, as they often spoke for other underdogs; it is perhaps relevant that three of the men condemned seem to have been comic poets.

Production

Since fifth-century comic poets put on a play for a particular competition and did not envisage future productions, an original script that later circulated as a text for readers contained only the words, with few if any attributions of lines to speakers and no stage directions. These had to be inferred from the words of the text itself, so that all editions and translations, ancient and modern, differ to some extent in reconstructing the theatricality of the text. This means that anyone reading or performing an ancient comedy has a perfect right to bring the text to life in any way that seems appropriate: we have no information external to the text itself about how lines were originally distributed or performed, or about the original action on-stage and in the orchestra. Thus there can be no "authentic" productions of ancient comedies, only productions that either strive, to a greater or lesser degree, to approximate what little we know of performance conditions at the time of their original production, or productions that modernize a play, like Stephen Sondheim's musical version of *Frogs*, in which Shakespeare and Shaw replace Aeschylus and Euripides. In either case it is pointless to argue about "authenticity": in the end only satisfied spectators really count.

In this translation I assign speakers who seem to be the likeliest candidates for given lines; the reader is free to differ. I do not, however, supply stage-directions in the text itself: one of the pleasures of reading or performing an ancient comedy is imagining how it might be realized in action, so I hesitate to put my own imagination in the way of a reader's, an actor's, or a director's. But I do occasionally draw attention, in the notes, to likely action that is not quite obvious from the words of the text.

We do know some facts about fifth-century comic theater, however, and there is no harm in reviewing them for their historical interest.

Although Aristophanes' comedies are highly sophisticated as poetry and as drama, they nevertheless respected some ancient Dionysiac traditions that we should bear in mind if we want to respond to the characters in historical perspective. The actors wore masks, made of cork or papier-mâché, that covered the entire head. These were generic (young man, old woman, etc.) but might occasionally be special, like portrait-masks of prominent citizens (as in the case of Socrates in *Clouds*) or (as in *Birds*) of animals or gods. Although the characters' clothing was generically suited to their dramatic identities, mostly contemporary Greeks, there were several features that made them unmistakably comic: wherever possible, the costumes accommodated the traditional comic features of big stomach and rump and (for male characters) the grotesque costume penis called the phallos, made of leather, either dangling or erect as appropriate, and circumcised in the case of outlandish barbarians. Apparently by comic convention, male characters appearing without a phallos were marked as being in some way unmanly. And, as in every other dramatic genre, all roles were played by men. Even the naked females who often appear on stage, typically in the traditionally festive ending, were men wearing body-stockings to which false breasts and genitalia were attached. But the convention of all-male actors does not mean that Old Comedy was a kind of drag show: the same convention applied to all other kinds of drama as well (as it still did in Shakespeare's time), and nowhere in our comic texts is any female character ever understood to be anything but the character she is supposed to be, never a male playing a female.

The city supplied an equal number of actors to each competing poet, probably three, and these actors played all the speaking roles. In *Birds*, for example, there are twenty-two speaking roles, but the text's entrances and exits are so arranged that three actors can play them all. Some plays do, however, require a fourth (or even a fifth) actor in small roles. Perhaps in given years the allotment changed, or novices were periodically allowed to take small parts, or the poet or producer could add extra actors at his own expense.

In the orchestra ("dancing space") was a chorus of twenty-four men who sang and danced to the accompaniment of an aulos, a wind instrument that had two recorder-like pipes played simultaneously by a specially costumed player; and there could be other instruments as well. Like actors, members of the chorus wore masks and costumes appropriate to their dramatic identity. There could be dialogue between the chorus-leader and the actors on-stage, but the chorus as a whole only sings and dances. There was no ancient counterpart to the "choral speaking" often heard in modern performances of Greek drama. The choral songs of comedy were in music and language usually in a popular style, though serious styles were often parodied, and the dancing was expressive, adding a visual dimension to the words and music.

The stage-area was a slightly raised platform behind the large orchestra. Behind it was a wooden two-story building called the *skene* ("tent", from which our word "scene"). It had two or three doors at stage-level, windows at the second story, and a roof on which actors could appear. On the roof was a crane called the *mechane* ("machine"), on which actors could fly above the stage (as gods, for example, whence the Latin expression *deus ex machina*, "god from the machine"). Another piece of permanent equipment was a wheeled platform called the *ekkyklema* ("device for rolling out"), on which actors and scenery could be wheeled on-stage from the *skene* to reveal "interior" action. A painted or otherwise decorated plywood facade could be attached to the *skene* if a play (or scene) required it, and movable props and other scenery were used as needed. Since plays were performed in daylight in a large outdoor amphitheater, all entrances and exits of performers and objects took place in full view of the spectators. All in all, more demand was made on the spectators' imagination than in modern illusionistic theater, so that performers must often tell the spectators what they are supposed to see.

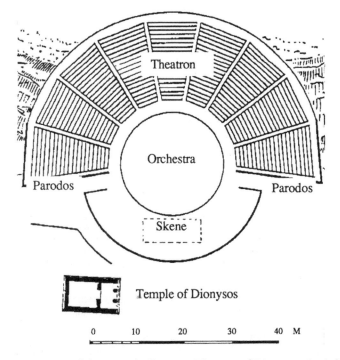

A Reconstruction of the Fourth-Century Theater of Dionysos in Athens

A fifth-century comedy was played through without intermission, the performance probably lasting about two hours. The usual structure of a comedy was a Prologue (actors); the Parodos, or entry, of the chorus into the orchestra (chorus); an Agon, or contest (actors and chorus); the Parabasis, or self-revelation, of the chorus (chorus-leader and chorus); and a series of episodes (actors) articulated by choral songs (chorus). In some plays, like *Frogs*, there can be a second parabasis and/or a second agon. In this translation I have supplied appropriate divisions of the action (see below), but performers should, as always, feel free to arrange their own performance as they see fit.

Frogs and Its Time

Frogs was produced at the Lenaea of 405 by Philonides, an old associate of Aristophanes who had produced other plays for him. It won the first prize; Phrynichus was second with *Muses* (whose title suggests an artistic, and perhaps literary, theme) and Platon third with *Cleophon* (a leading politician of the time who is also attacked in *Frogs*).

According to the surviving Hypothesis (the ancient summary of the play's action), which cites as its authority Aristotle's pupil Dicaearchus, the city awarded *Frogs* the unique distinction of being restaged "because of its parabasis," and the ancient *Life of Aristophanes*, probably also deriving its information from Dicaearchus, informs us that Aristophanes was "officially commended and crowned with a wreath of sacred olive, considered equal in honor to a gold crown, for the lines he had spoken in *Frogs* about the disenfranchised" (lines 686 ff.). The decree that awarded the commendation and restaging must have been passed after the autumn of 405, when by the decree of Patrocleides the Athenians enacted the measure for which Aristophanes had appealed in the parabasis, but before the overthrow of the democracy in the spring of 404, when an appeal for equal civic rights would have been ill received. And so the play will have been restaged at the Lenaea of 404. For the restaging Aristophanes probably made only a few minor changes: lines 1251-60, 1431a-b, and 1437-53 seem to contain alternative versions of the text, but passages that would have been inappropriate at the time of the restaging remain, and there are no references to the events of early 404.

In *Frogs* Dionysus, the wine god and patron deity of the Athenian dramatic festivals, is a major character and the only one who is involved in the action throughout the play. In the first half of the play he is the anti-heroic and burlesque figure long familiar in comedy and satyr drama. In Cratinus' *Dionysus as Paris* (*Dionysalexandros*) he had taken the place of Paris as judge of the famous mythical beauty contest between Athena, Hera, and Aphrodite (with Helen as the prize); in Eupolis' *Taxiarchs* the Athenian admiral Phormio unsuccessfully tried to teach him to be a sailor-warrior, as in Aristomenes' *Dionysus the Athlete* he had been trained as an athlete. In the second half of the play he arbitrates a contest between the poets Aeschylus and Euripides for pre-eminence in the art of tragedy.

The play begins with Dionysus, disguised as his half-brother, the great hero Heracles, traveling to the underworld with his cheeky slave, Xanthias, in order to retrieve his favorite tragic poet, the recently deceased Euripides. The first part of the play (1-673) chronicles their *katabasis* (descent to the underworld): a meeting with the real Heracles to obtain directions; Dionysus' voyage across the lake that leads to the underworld, ineptly rowing Charon's skiff and engaging in song with a chorus of frogs (a familiar feature of lakes and apt figures for a musical contest); Dionysus' attempts to disguise his cowardice in the face of underworld bogeys; the entry of the main chorus of Eleusinian Initiates, who live near the palace of Pluto, god of the underworld; several scenes of the sort that typically occur in the second part of a comedy, after the parabasis, in which Dionysus attempts to avoid the predicaments that await him upon arrival by exchanging his disguise with Xanthias; and finally Dionysus' admission into Pluto's palace.

After the parabasis, there is a conversation between Xanthias and a slave of Pluto's that amounts to a second prologue introducing a new situation: Dionysus has been recruited by Pluto to judge a contest for the underworld Chair of Tragedy between Aeschylus, its long-time incumbent, and Euripides, who upon arrival has laid claim to preeminence in the art. Much of the ensuing contest focuses on the rivals' poetic techniques, with detailed critiques of actual passages from their plays and parody of their characteristic styles. But Aeschylus and Euripides also emerge as representatives of the character, both poetic and civic, of their respective eras, and the decisive test turns on which poet is more able to effect "the salvation of Athens and the continuation of her choral festivals" (1418-19). On this criterion Dionysus chooses Aeschylus, and Pluto tells him that he may take Aeschylus with him back to Athens; Sophocles, also recently deceased, will hold the Chair of Tragedy in his absence and make sure that Euripides never sits in it. The Chorus of Eleusinian Initiates lead Dionysus and Aeschylus off in a torchlight procession recalling the inspirational finale of Aeschylus' *Oresteia*.

Beyond being a landmark in the history of literary criticism, *Frogs* embraces two transcendent issues, the decline of Athens as a great power, as the long Peloponnesian War (431-404) approached its end, and the decline of tragedy as a great form of art, with the recent deaths of the last two preeminent tragedians. Aristophanes connects these two issues by portraying tragic poets as both exemplifying and shaping the moral and civic character of their times. Aristophanes' solution to both — the resurrection of Aeschylus from the dead — is at once pessimistic and optimistic: if there were no longer any living poets who could inspire the Athenians to greatness, at least the works of Aeschylus lived on and might inspire the Athenians to recapture the virtues that had made their city preeminent in his day.

The decline of Athens and its musical culture were hardly new themes in the comedies of Aristophanes and his contemporaries, and the remedy of resurrecting great men of the past had recently figured in at least two of them: in Eupolis' *Demes* (412) the hero Pyronides brings back four great leaders (Solon, Miltiades, Aristeides, and Pericles), and in Aristophanes' *Gerytades* (c. 408) the poets of Athens send an embassy to the underworld, presumably to resurrect the goddess Poetry (cf. fr. 591.85-86); Pherecrates' *Crapataloi* (date unknown but probably before *Frogs*) may have been similar, since Aeschylus' ghost is a character, and someone is told what to expect in the underworld (fragments 86, 100). But these themes had taken on a special urgency at the time of *Frogs*, for a shortage both of reliable manpower and trustworthy leadership threatened Athenian prospects for surviving the war, just as the passing of Euripides and Sophocles threatened the future of Athens' greatest art form.

The Athenians' military and political situation had not improved since the Sicilian disaster of 413 and now threatened to deteriorate. The naval victory at Arginusae the previous summer had given Athens control of the Aegean but came at a crippling cost: after all available manpower had been mobilized, including slaves enlisted as rowers on the promise of freedom and even citizenship (this extraordinary action was no doubt a factor in the unusually prominent and complex characterization of Xanthias in our play, cf. especially lines 33, 693-99), twenty-five ships and some five thousand men were lost, and in the subsequent recriminations all eight commanders were rashly (and illegally) condemned to death by the Assembly. In their ensuing remorse the Athenians compounded this mistake by denying commands to those they held responsible for the condemnations, including two exceptionally qualified captains, Theramenes and Thrasybulus. Alcibiades, who had capably led the Athenian naval effort since 411, had gone into voluntary exile in 407, and the question of his recall figures prominently in the decision between Aeschylus and Euripides (lines 1422-32). The men who had been disenfranchised for their association with the oligarchy of 411, and on whose behalf Aristophanes appeals in the parabasis, were still debarred from civic life. Meanwhile, the Peloponnesians had finally begun to receive significant financial support from Persia, while the Athenians' financial situation steadily worsened: they were unable to restore their fleet to its pre-Arginusae strength, and their traditional silver coinage, augmented by an emergency issue of gold coins made by melting down the plating on the Victory statues in the Parthenon, had to be spent abroad to pay military expenses, and to be replaced at home by an issue of silver-plated bronze coins.

But even in this perilous situation, the popular leader Cleophon managed to persuade the Athenians to reject the chance of a negotiated peace offered by Sparta after Arginusae, so that it is hardly surprising that the Athenians responded so warmly to the parabasis of *Frogs*, where the Chorus aptly upbraids them for choosing as leaders and fighters not the best men but the worst, just as they have traded their gold and silver coinage for base metal (686-705, 717-37).

Aristophanes considered the situation on the tragic stage to be comparable to the military situation, for Euripides had died early in 406 in his late seventies, and Sophocles a few months later in his early nineties. Both were international celebrities, and had long been considered the preeminent living masters of the art, with Aeschylus (who had died in the mid-450s) as the third member of the great tragic triad. But whereas the Athenians could redeem their political and military situation if they turned to the best people, who were still living among them and eager to serve (cf. line 699), no such choice was available in the case of tragic poets, for Dionysus can think of no worthy successors among those who remained (lines 71-97), so that the redemption of tragedy could only be found beyond the grave. There seems to have been some justice in Dionysus' appraisal of the prospects for tragedy, for even if the poets left in Athens were not as inferior as he claims, the fact remains that when revivals became part of the program at the City Dionysia in the early fourth century, only revivals of plays by Euripides and Sophocles are attested; Aeschylus had already (and uniquely) enjoyed this status during the fifth century.

The play assumes that Sophocles is dead, but that he is mentioned in only three detachable passages (lines 76-82, 786-94, and 1515-19) suggests that he died too late to be incorporated more fully into the plot. Presumably the play was conceived and largely completed when he was still alive, and Aristophanes added these passages to adjust for his death. He may well have had to remove some passages as well, for the original script would somehow have acknowledged the presence of the still-productive Sophocles among living poets. But this acknowledgement need not have been very detailed: in view of Sophocles' advanced age alone, Dionysus could simply have said, "there are no worthy poets left except Sophocles, and he won't be with us much longer." In any event, it is unlikely that Sophocles would have figured in the poetic contest even if he had died at the same time as Euripides: in contrast to Euripides, Sophocles had never been an attractive target in comedy for either personal caricature or poetic parody, whereas the contrast between Aeschylus and Euripides personally, poetically, and as representatives of their eras ideally suited Aristophanes' purposes.

The poetic contest in *Frogs* assumes that the spectators are familiar not only with dramatic literature (that is, drama primarily as texts as distinct from performances) but also with literary criticism, and that this familiarity was relatively recently acquired: as the Chorus says, "if you're afraid of any ignorance among the spectators, that they won't appreciate your subtleties of argument, don't worry about that, because things are no longer that way: they're veterans, and each one has a book and knows the fine points" (lines 1108-14). Critiques of poets and their poetry, including metaphorical descriptions of their qualities and techniques, had long been a feature the Greek poetic tradition, and during the latter half of the fifth century became increasingly refined, as did the study of language and its communicative powers generally: the portrayal of poets and criticism of their works, both formal and through parody, was a staple subject of comedy, as it had been in earlier times (*Contest of Homer and Hesiod*, for example, foreshadows the contest in *Frogs*); the language, style, and persuasive techniques of oratory and poetry (including the role of poets not only as providers of emotional and aesthetic pleasure but also as teachers and advisors) among the principal interests of sophistic thinkers and writers; and the increasing circulation and study of books had begun to create a more sophisticated awareness of poetry as literature, and of criticism as a formal approach to it. *Frogs* both reflects this development and contributed to it.

The following scheme outlines the main structural divisions of the play.

SCENE 1: PROLOGUE (1-208)
(*Xanthias, Dionysus, Heracles, Corpse, Pallbearers, Charon*)
CONTEST WITH FROGS (209-268)
(*Chorus of Frogs, Dionysus*)

The Translation

This translation is designed for both readers and performers and presupposes no knowledge of classical Greece or classical Greek theater. I have translated the Greek text into contemporary American verse, speakability being the principal stylistic criterion, and line by line, so as to give a sense of the play's original scope and pace. The Greek text is that of my Loeb Classical Library edition, in places incorporating improvements made by Nigel G. Wilson in his new edition of Aristophanes' plays (Oxford 2007), and for textual and interpretive matters of all kinds I am much indebted to the editions with commentary by Kenneth J. Dover (Oxford 1993) and Alan H. Sommerstein (Warminster 1996).

The conventions of Aristophanic comedy included sharp satire, rough personal attack, and the frank portrayal and discussion of religion, politics, and sex (including nudity and obscenity). Although these features are less in evidence in *Frogs* than in most of our other plays by Aristophanes, I have tried to reproduce them as accurately as possible within my general guideline of faithfulness to the original and easy intelligibility. Some readers may be surprised or even offended to find such material in a classical work, but it is there, and not to translate it would be to falsify the plays. After all, one of Aristophanes' chief aims was to make humor of important dimensions of human life and society, while at the same time encouraging his audience to think about them in ways discouraged, or even forbidden, outside the comic theater. The issue of freedom of speech and thought (especially religious and moral thought) is especially relevant to Aristophanes' plays, and it is important to bear in mind that one of the hallmarks of Aristophanic comedy is to encourage us to question the status quo. For those made uncomfortable by such provocative theater, Aristophanes' plays provide an opportunity to ask themselves why.

Bibliography

Editions of the Plays with English Translation

Henderson, Jeffrey. *Aristophanes*. 5 volumes (Loeb Classical Library: Cambridge, MA 1998-2007)

Sommerstein, Alan H. *The Comedies of Aristophanes*. 12 volumes (Aris & Phillips: Warminster 1980-2002)

General Treatments of Aristophanic Comedy

Arnott, P. *Greek Scenic Conventions in the Fifth Century B.C.* (Oxford 1962)

Bowie, A.M. *Aristophanes. Myth, Ritual and Comedy* (Cambridge 1993)

Cartledge, P. *Aristophanes and his Theatre of the Absurd* (London 1990)

Davidson, J. N. *Courtesans and Fishcakes: The Consuming Passions of Classical Athens* (London 1997)

Dobrov, G.W., ed. *The City as Comedy. Society and Representation in Athenian Drama* (Chapel Hill and London 1997)

Dover, K.J. *Aristophanic Comedy* (California 1972)

Ehrenberg, V. *The People of Aristophanes. A Sociology of Old Attic Comedy*[3] (New York 1962)

Harriott, R.M. *Aristophanes, Poet and Dramatist* (Baltimore 1986)

Harvey, F. D. and Wilkins, J. eds. *The Rivals of Aristophanes* (London/ Swansea 2000)

Henderson, J. *The Maculate Muse: Obscene Language in Attic Comedy*[2] (Oxford 1990)

Hubbard, T.K. *The Mask of Comedy. Aristophanes and the Intertextual Parabasis* (Ithaca 1991)

MacDowell, D.M. *Aristophanes and Athens* (Oxford 1995)

McLeish, K. *The Theatre of Aristophanes* (New York 1980)

Moulton, C. *Aristophanic Poetry* (Hypomnemata 68: Göttingen 1981)

Pelling, C. B. R. *Literary Texts and the Greek Historian* (London 2000), pp. 123-63

Reckford, K.J. *Aristophanes' Old-and-New Comedy* (Chapel Hill 1987)

Russo, C.F. *Aristophanes, an Author for the Stage* (London 1994)

Silk, M. S. *Aristophanes and the Definition of Comedy* (Oxford 2000)

Solomos, A. *The Living Aristophanes* (Ann Arbor 1974)

Sommerstein, A.H. et al., eds. *Tragedy, Comedy and the Polis* (Bari 1993)

Whitman, C.H. *Aristophanes and the Comic Hero* (Cambridge MA 1964)

Winkler, J.J. and Zeitlin, F.I., eds. *Nothing to Do With Dionysos? Athenian Drama in its Social Context* (Princeton 1990)

The Production of Attic Comedy

Csapo, E. and Slater, W.J. *The Context of Ancient Drama* (Ann Arbor 1995)

Green, J.R. *Theatre in Ancient Greek Society* (London and New York 1994)

Hall, E. and Wrigley, A. *Aristophanes in Performance, 421 BC – AD 2007: Peace, Birds and Frogs* (Legenda: Oxford 2008)

Pickard-Cambridge, A.W. *Dithyramb, Tragedy and Comedy*, rev. by T.B.L. Webster (Oxford 1962)

_____ *The Dramatic Festivals of Athens*, rev. by J. Gould and D.M. Lewis (Oxford 1968, rev. 1988)

Rothwell, K. S., Jr. *Nature, Culture, and the Origins of Greek Comedy* (Cambridge 2007)

Sifakis, G. *Parabasis and Animal Choruses* (London 1971)

Slater, N. W. *Spectator Politics: Metatheatre and Performance in Aristophanes* (Philadelphia 2002)

Stone, L.M. *Costume in Aristophanic Comedy* (New York 1981)

Taplin, O. *Comic Angels and Other Approaches to Greek Drama through Vase-Paintings* (Oxford 1993)

Van Steen, G. A. H. *Venom in Verse: Aristophanes in Modern Greece* (Princeton 2000)

Walcot, P. *Greek Drama in its Theatrical and Social Context* (Cardiff 1976)

Wilson, P. *The Athenian Institution of the Khoregia. The Chorus, the City and the Stage* (Cambridge 2003)

Further Reading about Frogs

Allison, R. H. "Amphibian Ambiguities: Aristophanes and his *Frogs*," *Greece and Rome* 30 (1983) 8-20

Edmonds, R. G. *Myths of the Underworld Journey: Plato, Aristophanes, and the "Orphic" Gold Tablets* (Cambridge 2004)

Konstan, D. *Greek Comedy and Ideology* (New York 1995), Ch. 4

Lada-Richards, I. *Initiating Dionysus: Ritual and Theatre in Aristophanes* (Oxford 1999)

Marshall, C. W. "Amphibian Ambiguities Answered," *Echos du monde classique* 40 (1996) 251-65

Segal, C. P. "The Character and Cults of Dionysus and the Unity of the *Frogs*," *Harvard Studies in Classical Philology* 65 (1961) 207-42

Aristophanes: Frogs

CHARACTERS

SPEAKING CHARACTERS

Xanthias, slave of Dionysus[1]
Dionysus
Heracles
Corpse
Charon
Aeacus, doorman of Pluto
Maid of Persephone

Innkeeper
Plathane, innkeeper
Slave of Pluto
Pluto
Euripides
Aeschylus

SILENT CHARACTERS

Donkey
Pallbearers
Maids of the Innkeepers
Slaves of Pluto
Scythian policemen (Ditylas, Scebylas, Pardocas)
Muse of Euripides
Persephone

CHORUS of Frogs
CHORUS of Eleusinian Initiates

---

1   "Light-Haired," a common slave-name.

SCENE I: PROLOGUE (1-208)

(Xanthias, Dionysus, Heracles, Corpse, Pallbearers, Charon)

Enter DIONYSUS and XANTHIAS from the side. Dionysus, disguised as Heracles, wears a lionskin over his saffron gown and carries a club; Xanthias rides a Donkey and carries baggage suspended from a pole that rests on his shoulder. They make their way toward the stage house.

Xanthias
> Hey master, how about some of the usual stuff
> that always gets a laugh from the audience?

Dionysus
> Why sure, whatever you like, except "I'm hard pressed!"
> Watch out for that one; by now it gets only a groan.

Xanthias
> Then something urbane?

Dionysus
>   Except for "I'm getting crushed!"   5

Xanthias
> Well, how about that really funny one?

Dionysus
>   Sure,
> go right ahead: only please, not the one where—

Xanthias
>   you mean—

Dionysus
> where you shift your baggage and say you need to shit.

Xanthias
> I can't even say I've got such a load on me
> that if someone doesn't relieve me my butt will erupt?   10

Dionysus
> Please don't, I beg you! Wait till I need to puke.

Xanthias
> Then why did I have to come humping all this baggage,
> if I can't do any of the stuff that Phrynichus
> is always doing? Lycis and Ameipsias too:

people hump baggage in every one of their comedies.[2]   15

Dionysus
  Just don't, because when I'm in the audience
  whenever I see one of those sophisticated bits,
  I go back home more than a whole year older.

Xanthias
  Then this neck of mine is truly triple-jinxed:
  it's getting crushed but can't make a funny comment.   20

Dionysus
  How's that for arrogance and being spoiled rotten!
  After I, none other than Dionysus son of Flagon,[3]
  have toiled ahead on foot and let him ride,
  so he wouldn't get tired or have to bear a load.

Xanthias
  Aren't I bearing one?

Dionysus
                          How can you bear when you're riding?   25

Xanthias
  I'm bearing *this*.

Dionysus
                    How?

Xanthias
                          Quite unbearably!

Dionysus
  But doesn't the donkey bear what you are bearing?

Xanthias
  Not what I've got here and bear myself, it doesn't.

Dionysus
  But how can you be bearing, when something else bears you?

Xanthias
  I haven't a clue—but this shoulder of mine is hard pressed!   30

Dionysus
  OK, since you deny that the donkey's helping you,
  pick up the donkey and take your turn carrying *him*.

---

2   Three of Aristophanes' comic competitors; at this festival Phrynichus was
     competing against *Frogs* with his *Muses* and would win second prize.
3   Instead of "son of Zeus," alluding to Dionysus' role as wine-god.

Xanthias

Oh blast my luck, why wasn't I in the sea battle?
Then I'd be telling *you* to go to hell.[4]

Dionysus

Dismount, you scamp! Here I stand at the very door   35
that was supposed to be the first stop of my trip. (*knocking*)
Boy! Boy, I say, boy![5]

HERACLES is heard from within, then opens the door.

Heracles

Who banged on the door? He assaulted it like a centaur,
whoever— Say now, what's *this* supposed to be?

Dionysus

Boy!

Xanthias

What is it?

Dionysus

Did you see that?

Xanthias

See what?   40

Dionysus

How scared he was!

Xanthias

Sure, scared that you've lost your mind.

Heracles

I swear to god, I simply can't stop laughing!
I'm biting my lip, but still I can't help laughing.

Dionysus

Come here, my man; I'd like a word with you.

Heracles

I'm sorry, but I can't shake off this laughter.   45
It's seeing that lionskin atop a yellow gown.[6]

---

4   The Athenian fleet that was victorious at Arginusae the previous summer had
been manned by a great levy that included slaves, who were then rewarded
with freedom.

5   The conventional way of referring to a slave.

6   Normally a woman's festive garment but regularly worn by Dionysus, sometimes
in combination with masculine clothing.

What's the idea? Why a war club with lady's boots?
Where on earth have you been?

Dionysus

Serving topside with Cleisthenes.[7]

Heracles
And did you engage?

Dionysus

Oh yes, and I also sank
some enemy ships, maybe twelve or thirteen of them.   50

Heracles
You two?

Dionysus

So help me Apollo.

Xanthias

And then I woke up.

Dionysus
Well anyway, as I was up on deck
reading *Andromeda*[8] to myself, a sudden longing
struck my heart, you can't imagine how hard.

Heracles
A longing? How big?

Dionysus

Small, the size of Molon.[9]   55

Heracles
For a woman?

Dionysus

Nope.

Heracles

A boy, then?

Dionysus

Not in the slightest.

---

7 Perennially teased for passive homosexuality.

8 This play of Euripides had been produced in 412 and was parodied by
   Aristophanes the following year in *Women at the Thesmophoria* (lines
   1015-1135).

9 A famous actor and, according to ancient tradition, a large man.

Heracles
For a man, then?

Dionysus
                    Ah ah!

Heracles
                              Did you do it with Cleisthenes?

Dionysus
Don't tease me, brother;[10] I'm truly in a very bad way.
That's how thoroughly this passion is messing me up.

Heracles
What kind of passion, little brother?

Dionysus
                                        It's hard to put into words,   60
but I'll try to explain it to you by analogy.
Have you ever had a sudden craving for minestrone?

Heracles
Minestrone? Oh my, thousands of times in my life!

Dionysus
Am I being clear, or should I express it another way?

Heracles
No problem with minestrone; I get the point.   65

Dionysus
Well, that's the kind of longing that's eating me up —
for Euripides.

Heracles
              You mean, even dead and all?

Dionysus
And nobody on earth can persuade me not
to go after him.

Heracles
                To go even below to Hades?

Dionysus
By heaven, even if there's somewhere below that.   70

---

10   Dionysus and Heracles were both sons of Zeus respectively by Semele and
     Alcmene.

Heracles

What is it you want?

Dionysus

                     I need a talented poet,
"for some are gone, and those that live are bad."[11]

Heracles

How so? Isn't Iophon alive?[12]

Dionysus

                     Yes, and he's the only
class act left, that is, if he really is one;
for I'm not exactly sure how that stands either.   75

Heracles

If you're really set on resurrecting someone,
then why not Sophocles instead of Euripides?

Dionysus

No, first I want to get Iophon by himself
without Sophocles and evaluate what he produces.
Besides, Euripides is a slippery character   80
and would probably even help me pull off an escape,
while Sophocles was mild here and will be mild there.

Heracles

And where is Agathon?[13]

Dionysus

                     He's gone and left me,
An excellent poet and very much missed by his friends.[14]

Heracles

Where on earth to, poor thing?

Dionysus

                     To party with the Blest.   85

---

11   From Euripides' *Oeneus* (fragment 565).

12   A son of Sophocles and a successful tragic poet.

13   Agathon, victorious in his debut in 416 (commemorated in Plato's *Symposium*) and
      famous both for his innovative style and his personal beauty, had left Athens
      with his lover Pausanias for the court of Archelaus of Macedon around 408; he
      was portrayed in Aristophanes' *Women at the Thesmophoria* (produced in 411).

14   Or, with a variant reading, "by the wise."

Heracles
And what about Xenocles?[15]

Dionysus
                    To hell with *him*!

Heracles
And Pythangelus?[16]

Xanthias
                    But nary a word about me,
though my shoulder here's getting ever so badly bruised?

Heracles
But aren't there other poets here, lads busy
composing tragedies by the tens of thousands   90
and out-blabbering Euripides by a mile?

Dionysus
All those are cast-offs and merely empty chatter,
choirs of swallows, wreckers of their art,
who maybe get a chorus and are soon forgotten,
after having their single piss upon Tragedy.   95
But if you look for a potent poet, one who could utter
a lordly phrase, you won't find any left.

Heracles
What do you mean, "potent"?

Dionysus
                    Potent, as in one
who can give voice to something adventuresome,
like "Aether, Bedchamber of Zeus,"[17] or "Time's Foot,"[18]   100
or a heart unwilling to swear on ritual victims,
and a tongue forsworn separately from the heart.[19]

Heracles
You like that stuff?

---

15   A son of the tragic poet Carcinus who defeated Euripides' Trojan trilogy in
     415.

16   Otherwise unknown.

17   Misquoting Euripides' *Wise Melanippe* (fragment 487), "Aether, Zeus' abode."

18   Euripides' *Alexander* (fragment 42), *Bacchae*, line 889.

19   Paraphrasing a notorious line from Euripides' *Hippolytus* (612), "My tongue has
     sworn, but my heart is not under oath."

Dionysus

             Me like it? I'm crazy about it!

Heracles

    It's pure blarney; you know it as well as I do.

Dionysus

    Don't manage my mind,[20] but mind your own business.   105

Heracles

    Oh come on now, it's obviously utter rubbish.

Dionysus

    Oh stick to your specialty: eating!

Xanthias

                Not a word about me!

Dionysus

    Well, as to the reason I've come here wearing this outfit
    in imitation of you is so you'll tell me
    about those friends of yours who put you up   110
    that time when you went after Cerberus,[21]
    in case I need them. Tell me about the harbors,
    the bakeries, whorehouses, rest areas, directions,
    the springs, roads, cities, places to stay, the landladies
    with the fewest bedbugs.

Xanthias

                Not a word about me!   115

Heracles

    You madcap, would you dare to go there too?[22]

Dionysus

    Just drop that subject, and give me the directions,
    my quickest route on down to Hades, and mind
    you don't give me one that's too hot or too cold.

Heracles

    All right, which one shall I give you first? Let's see.   120
    Well, there's one via rope and bench: you hang yourself.

---

20 Euripides' *Andromeda* (fragment 144).

21 The three-headed watchdog of Hades, fetched up by Heracles in the last of his labors.

22 In portraying this as Dionysus' first trip to the underworld, Aristophanes apparently ignores the myths of his trip there to rescue his mother Semele.

Dionysus
Oh stop it, that way's stifling.

Heracles
                              Well, there's a shortcut
that's well-beaten—in a mortar.

Dionysus
                                          You mean hemlock?

Heracles
Exactly.

Dionysus
                    That's a chill and wintry way!   125
It quickly freezes your shins as hard as ice.

Heracles
How about quick and downhill?

Dionysus
                                        Sure: I'm not much for hiking.

Heracles
Then stroll to the Cerameicus[23]—

Dionysus
                                And then do what?

Heracles
climb up the tower, the high one—

Dionysus
                                And then do what?   130

Heracles
You watch the start of the torch race from up there,
and when the spectators start to cry "they're off,"
then off *you* go as well.

Dionysus
                          Off where?

Heracles
                                  Off down!

Dionysus
But I'd be wasting a pair of brain croquettes.
I'd rather not stroll that route.

---

23 "Potters' Town," a district of Athens extending northwest of the Agora.

Heracles
> Then how will you go?   135

Dionysus
The same way *you* went.

Heracles
> Well, that's a lengthy voyage.
First of all you'll come to a very large lake,
quite bottomless.

Dionysus
> Then how will I get across it?

Heracles
An ancient mariner will ferry you across
in a skiff no bigger than *this*, for a fare of two obols.[24]   140

Dionysus
Amazing the power those two obols everywhere have!
How did they get down there?

Heracles
> Theseus brought them.[25]
After that, you'll see an infinity of serpents and beasts
most frightful.

Dionysus
> Don't try to shock or scare me off:
you'll not deter me.

Heracles
> Then you'll see a lot   145
of mud and ever-flowing shit; and therein lies
anyone who ever wronged a stranger,
or snatched back a boy's fee while screwing him,
or beat his mother up, or socked his father
right in the mouth, or falsely swore an oath,   150
or had someone copy out a speech by Morsimus.[26]

---

24 The traditional fare was one obol; here "two obols" probably refers to the two-obol public dole introduced by the politician Cleophon in 410; some have thought that it refers to the price of a theater ticket, but then "everywhere" (i.e., not only in Athens) is hard to explain.

25 The underworld journey of Theseus, an Athenian hero, was well known and was dramatized in the tragedy *Perithous* (date of production unknown), which in antiquity was attributed to Critias but alternatively to Euripides.

26 Son of the tragic poet Philocles and great-nephew of Aeschylus; ridiculed elsewhere in comedy as a bad tragedian.

Dionysus
> And by heaven, we should also add to these
> anyone who learned that war dance by Cinesias.[27]

Heracles
> And next, a breath of pipes will waft about you,
> and there'll be brilliant sunlight, just like ours,   155
> and myrtle groves, and happy festive bands
> of men and women, and a great clapping of hands.

Dionysus
> And who are those people?

Heracles
>   The Initiates.

Xanthias
> And I'm the damn donkey who carries out the Mysteries!
> But I'm not going to put up with it any longer.   160

Heracles
> They'll tell you everything you need to know.
> They live beside the road that you'll be taking,
> Right by the very gates of Pluto's[28] palace.
> So bon voyage, my brother.

> *HERACLES goes inside.*

Dionysus
>   And best to you as well.
> And as for you, pick up that baggage again.   165

Xanthias
> Before I've even put it down?

Dionysus
>   And make it snappy.

Xanthias
> I won't! Instead, please hire someone, someone
> being laid to rest, who's headed in the same direction.

---

27   The dance in full armor (*pyrriche*) was a prestigious competition at the quadrennial Athenian festival of the Panathenaea, which had been held the previous summer. Cinesias was a contemporary dithyrambic poet much ridiculed in comedy for his wasted physique and airy, avante-garde music.

28   God of the underworld, who lived there in a palace with his wife, Persephone, daughter of the grain-goddess Demeter.

Dionysus
What if I can't find one?

Xanthias
                    Then take *me*.

Enter Pallbearers, bearing a CORPSE on a bier.

Dionysus
                              Good suggestion.
And look, here's a corpse they're bearing off right now.   170
You there, yes I mean you, the deceased one.
Hey buddy, want to haul some bags to Hades?

Corpse
How many?

Dionysus
            These here.

Corpse
                    Will you pay two drachmas?

Dionysus
Certainly not that much.

Corpse
                    Move along, bearers.

Dionysus
Hold on there, fella, maybe we can work something out.   175

Corpse
Put down two drachmas then, or else shut up.

Dionysus
Here's one and a half.

Corpse
                    I'd sooner live again!

CORPSE is borne away.

Xanthias
Pretty arrogant, the bastard. Well, to hell with him!
I'll do it myself.

Dionysus
                    You are a fine gentleman.
Let's head for the boat.

CHARON punts a wheeled boat into the orchestra and over to the stage.

Charon[29]

    Woo-op, lay her alongside.   180

Dionysus
    What's this?

Xanthias
    What's that? A lake.

Dionysus
        Why yes it is,
the very lake he told us of, and I see a boat there too.

Xanthias
    Yes, by Poseidon, and that's Charon himself.

Dionysus
    Welcome Charon!

Xanthias
    Welcome, Charon!

Dionysus and Xanthias
    Welcome Charon![30]

Charon
    Who's for release from all their cares and troubles?   185
    Who's for the Plain of Oblivion? For "Ocnus' Twinings"?[31]
    The Land of the Cerberians?[32] The buzzards? Taenarum?[33]

Dionysus
    Me.

Charon
    Then hurry aboard.

Dionysus
    Where are you headed?

---

29 Traditionally imagined as wearing a short garment that left one shoulder bare and a conical hat.

30 The triple greeting of Charon parodies a scene in Achaeus' lost satyr play, *Aethon*.

31 A famous painting by Polygnotus at Delphi depicted Ocnus in the underworld, plaiting a rope that a donkey keeps eating away; and he was known elsewhere in Athenian drama.

32 A people mentioned in Sophocles (fragment 1060) and (a variant) in *Odyssey* 11.14; here appropriately suggesting Cerberus.

33 The middle of the three promontories at the southern tip of the Peloponnese (now Cape Matapan), where Heracles entered the underworld to fetch Cerberus.

Charon
To the buzzards!³⁴

Dionysus
Really?

Charon
Surely, just for you.
Now get aboard!

Dionysus
(*to Xanthias*)
Come on, boy.

Charon
I'm not taking   190
a slave, unless he fought for his hide in the sea battle.³⁵

Xanthias
No, actually, I couldn't be there; had the pinkeye.

Charon
Then you'd better start trekking around the lake, double-time.

Xanthias
Then where should I wait for you?

Charon
By the Withering Stone;
there's a rest stop there.

Dionysus
Did you get that?

Xanthias
Loud and clear.   195
Damn my luck, what crossed my path when I left the house?

Exit XANTHIAS by one of the parodoi.

Charon
Sit to the oar. If anyone else is sailing, hurry it up.
Hey you, what do you think you're doing?

Dionysus
Who, me? Why,
just sitting on the oar, right where you told me.

---

34   "Go to the buzzards" was the Athenian equivalent of "go to hell."
35   Arginusae.

Charon

Not *on* it! Sit right over here, fatso.   200

Dionysus

All right.

Charon

Now put out those hands and stretch your arms.

Dionysus

All right.

Charon

Quit playing around! Put your feet against the stretcher
and start rowing, gung-ho.

Dionysus

And how will I manage that?
I'm green, a landlubber, no Salaminian,
and I'm supposed to row?

Charon

Very easily, because you'll hear   205
some gorgeous songs as soon as you dip your oar.

Dionysus

Whose songs?

Charon

The Frog Swans; wonderful stuff.

Dionysus

Then give me the stroke.

Charon

O-op-op, O-op-op.

CONTEST WITH FROGS (209-268)

(Chorus of Frogs, Dionysus)

As the boat moves across the orchestra, a CHORUS OF FROGS enter by
the parodoi and begin to leap about, following the boat.

Frogs

Brekekekex koax koax,[36]	210
brekekekex koax koax!	
Children of lake and stream,	
let's voice a cry in concert	
with the pipes, our own euphonious	
song—koax koax—	
that once we sounded[37]	
for the Nysean son of Zeus,	215
Dionysus, in the Marshes,	
when the hungover throng of revellers	
on holy Pot Day	
reeled through my precinct.[38]	
brekekekex koax koax!	220

Dionysus

As for me, my butt's
getting sore, you koax koax.

Frogs

Brekekekex koax koax!

Dionysus

But I don't suppose you care.

Frogs

Brekekekex koax koax!   225

Dionysus

Blast you, and your koax too!
Yes, all you are is koax.

36 Since actual frogs can be heard to sing antiphonally, it may be that one group sings *brekekekex* and the other responds with *koax koax*.

37 The Frogs, being denizens of the underworld, are ghosts.

38 The sanctuary of Dionysus ("Nysean" refers to Nysa, the mythical mountain of his birth) in the Marshes (located southwest of the Acropolis) was the site of the Anthesteria festival, the second day of which (Pitchers) featured heavy drinking, and the third and final day (Pots) the dedication of the pitchers.

Frogs

Quite so, you busybody!
For the Muses skillful on the lyre cherish us,
and hornfoot Pan, who plays the tuneful reeds,   230
and Apollo the Harper delights in us too,
in thanks for the stalks that I grow
in lake water, as girding for his lyre.
Brekekekex koax koax!   235

Dionysus

But I've got blisters,
and my asshole's been seeping,
and pretty soon it'll burst out and say—

Frogs

Brekekekex koax koax!

Dionysus

Ah, you songful race,   240
do stop!

Frogs

Oh no, we'll sound off
even louder, if ever
on sunshiny days
we hopped through sedge
and reed, rejoicing in our song's
busily diving melodies,   245
or if ever in flight from Zeus' rain
we chimed underwater in the depths
a chorale spangled with
bubbly ploppifications.

Dionysus and Frogs

Brekekekex koax koax!   250

Dionysus

I'm borrowing this from you!

Frogs

What an awful thing to do!

Dionysus

But more awful for me, if this rowing   255
makes me burst apart.

Dionysus and Frogs
> Brekekekex koax koax!

Dionysus
> Wail away; what do I care?

Frogs
> In fact we'll bellow
> as loud as our gullets will stretch,
> all the livelong day!

Dionysus and Frogs
> Brekekekex koax koax!   260

Dionysus
> You won't beat me at this!

Frogs
> And you absolutely won't beat us!

Dionysus
> And you won't beat me either,
> never, for if need be I'll bellow
> all the livelong day, until   265
> I vanquish you at koax.
> Brekekekex koax koax!

> *Exit FROGS, unseen by Dionysus.*
> I knew I'd put a stop to that koax of yours!

SCENE II: ARRIVAL IN THE UNDERWORLD (269-322)

(Charon, Dionysus, Xanthias)

Charon
> Stop now, stop! Bring her alongside — with your oar.
> Off you go. Pay your fare!

Dionysus
>   Take your two obols.   270

> *CHARON punts away and exits by a parodos.*

> Xanthias! Where's Xanthias! Hey Xanthias!

Xanthias
> Yo!

Dionysus
Get over here!

*Re-enter XANTHIAS by the other parodos,
as having walked around the lake.*

Xanthias
Hello there, master.

Dionysus
What was your trip like?

Xanthias
Just darkness and mud.

Dionysus
So you must have seen those father beaters there
and those perjurers that he told us about.

Xanthias
Didn't you?   275

Dionysus
Sure I did, by Poseidon; and I can still see them.[39]
Well now, what's next?

Xanthias
We'd best be moving along,
for this is the place where he was mentioning
beasts, and awful ones.

Dionysus
And he'll regret it!
He was only bluffing, so that I'd be scared;   280
he knew that I'm a fighter and wanted no competition.
There's nothing as puffed up as Heracles.[40]
Why, I'd like nothing better than to encounter one
and chalk up an achievement worthy of this journey.

Xanthias
I know you would. And in fact I think I hear something.   285

Dionysus
Where? Where is it?

---

39   Looking out at the spectators.
40   Sophocles, *Philoctetes* fragment 788.1, substituting "Heracles" for "a man."

Xanthias

              Behind you.

Dionysus

                       Then get behind me!

Xanthias

But now it's in front.

Dionysus

                    Then get in front of me!

Xanthias

And now I see a really big beast.

Dionysus

                          What kind?

Xanthias

It's frightful! Anyway, it's a shape-shifter:
now it's a cow, now a mule, and now a woman,   290
very nice looking.

Dionysus

               Where is she? Let me at her!

Xanthias

Wait, she's not a woman any more, she's a bitch.

Dionysus

Then it must be Empusa![41]

Xanthias

                     Yes, her whole face is ablaze
with fire.

Dionysus

          And does she have a brazen leg?

Xanthias

Indeed she does, and the other one's made of dung,
I swear.

Dionysus

        Where can I run to?

Xanthias

                   Where can I?

---

41   A female bogey who played a role in the Eleusinian initiation ceremonies.

Dionysus

Priest,[42] save me, so I can come to your party![43]

Xanthias

Lord Heracles, we're done for!

Dionysus

Don't invoke me, man,
I beg you, and please don't use my name![44]

Xanthias

OK then: Dionysus!

Dionysus

That's even worse!   300

Xanthias

Begone now! Come here, master; over here.

Dionysus

What is it?

Xanthias

Buck up; everything's working out fine,
and we can say, along with Hegelochus,
"After the storm how weasily we sail."[45]
Empusa's gone.

Dionysus

Swear it!

Xanthias

So help me Zeus.   305

Dionysus

Swear it again!

Xanthias

By Zeus.

---

42   Addressed to the Priest of Dionysus, who sat in the front row of seats in the theater.

43   The party given by the producer for a victorious troupe after the performance.

44   It was popularly believed that evil spirits were directed to victims by knowing their name. Dionysus is still disguised as Heracles.

45   This actor played the lead in Euripides' play *Orestes* three years earlier and had thus mispronounced line 279 ("how easily"); other comic poets also recall his mishap.

Dionysus

        Swear!

Xanthias

          By Zeus.

Dionysus

  Good grief, how pale I went at the very sight of her!

Xanthias

  And how brown *this* went in fear on your behalf![46]

Dionysus

  Alas, whence have these woes befallen me?
  Whom of the gods shall I blame for my undoing?   310
  Aether, Bedchamber of Zeus? Or The Foot of Time?[47]

Xanthias

  Shhh.

Dionysus

     What is it?

Xanthias

        Didn't you hear?

Dionysus

            Hear what?

Xanthias

  The breath of pipes.

Dionysus

        I did, and a most mystic
  whiff of torches wafted over me.
  Let's hunker down right here and have a listen.   315

Chorus of Initiates

  (*off*)
   Iacchus, Iacchus![48]
   Iacchus, Iacchus!

Xanthias

  It's just as I thought, master: the initiates
  he told us about are frolicking hereabouts.

---

46 Pointing to his costume: Dionysus has soiled himself.

47 See line 100.

48 The Eleusinian cult name of Dionysus.

Yes, they're singing the Iacchus Hymn, the one by Diagoras.[49] 320

Dionysus

>I think so too. So our best course of action
>is to do nothing until we know for sure.

PARODOS OF THE CHORUS (323-459)

(Chorus of Initiates, Xanthias, Dionysus)

Enter CHORUS of male and female Initiates, wearing worn clothes and carrying torches.

Chorus

>Iacchus, dwelling exalted here in your abode,
>Iacchus, Iacchus,   325
>come to this meadow to dance
>with your reverent followers,
>brandishing about your brow
>>a fruitful, a burgeoning
>>garland of myrtle, and stamping   330
>>with bold foot in our licentious,
>>fun-loving worship,
>>that is richly endowed by the Graces, a dance
>>pure and holy to pious initiates.   335

Xanthias

>Most exalted lady, daughter of Demeter,
>what a nice aroma of pork wafted over me!

Dionysus

>Then be still, and you might get some sausage too.

Chorus

>Awaken blazing torches, tossing them in your hands,   340
>Iacchus, Iacchus,
>brilliant star of our nighttime rite!
>Lo, the meadow's ablaze with flame,
>and old men's knees are aleap   345

---

49 Diagoras of Melos was a noted atheist who by 414 had been outlawed from Athens with a price on his head for impugning the Mysteries in a lyric poem (not preserved). An alternative interpretation of the Greek is that they are singing the hymn " (as they go) through the agora" (*di' agoras*), which is to be preferred if we consider a joke to be inappropriate here.

as they shed their cares
and the long-drawn seasons of ancient years,
owing to your worship.
Now illuminate with torchlight   350
and lead forth to blooming meadowland
our dancing youth, o blest one!

Chorus Leader

All speak fair, and the following shall stand apart from our
    dances:
whoever is unfamiliar with such utterances as this, or harbors
    unclean attitudes,   355
or has never beheld or danced in the rites of the first-class Muses
nor been initiated in the Bacchic rites of bull-eating Cratinus'
    language,[50]
or enjoys clownish words from those who deliver them at the
    wrong time,
or forbears to resolve hateful factionalism and act peaceably
    toward fellow citizens,[51]
but foments and inflames it from desire for personal gain,   360
or as an official sells out the city when she's tossed on stormy
    seas,
or betrays a fortress or fleet, or is a goddamned collector
of 5% duties like Thorycion[52] and ships contraband from Aegina,
sending oar pads, flax, and pitch across to Epidaurus,[53]
or talks someone into supplying money for our adversaries'
    navy,   365
or shits on the offerings for Hecate while singing for
    dithyrambic choruses,[54]

---

50   Cratinus, here given a Dionysiac epithet (for he was famously a lover of
    wine), was the leading comic poet of the generation before Aristophanes; his
    Dionysalexandros ("Dionysus-Paris") may have been a model for *Frogs*, and last at-
    tested play, the autobiographical *Pytine* ("Wine-Bottle"), defeated Aristophanes'
    Clouds in 423.

51   Or, with the variant, "and act like a peaceable citizen."

52   In 413 these harbor duties on Athens' allies had replaced the tribute; according
    to the scholia, Thorycion was a taxiarch.

53   The island of Aegina was an Athenian settlement, and Epidaurus a contributor
    to the Peloponnesian navy.

54   A reference to the dithyrambic poet Cinesias, who had somehow been popularly
    connected with fouling (actually or metaphorically) the shrines of the goddess
    Hecate, which stood at intersections of three roads and where people left food-
    offerings on the last day of each month.

or is a politician who nibbles away the poets' honoraria
after being lampooned in a comedy during the ancestral rites of
    Dionysus.[55]
To these I proclaim, and proclaim again, and indeed thrice
    proclaim:
stand apart from the initiates' dances; but you[56] awaken the song
and our nightlong revels, which befit this festival.   371

Chorus

    Move on now boldly, everyone,
    to the lap of the flowery
    meadows, stamping the ground
    and jesting
    and frolicking and mocking;   375
    you've breakfasted well enough!
    So step out and be sure you exalt
    the Savior Goddess[57] in fine fashion,
    hymning her with your voices,
    she who vows to safeguard
    our land through the ages,   380
    despite what Thorycion wants.

Chorus Leader

Come now, celebrate in another form of song the queen of
    bounteous harvests,
the goddess Demeter, adorning her with holy hymns.

Chorus

    (*strophe*)
    Demeter, lady of pure rites,
    stand beside us   385
    and keep your chorus safe;
    and may I safely frolic and dance
    all the livelong day.
    (*antistrophe*)
    And may I utter much that's funny,
    and also much that's serious,   390
    and may I frolic and jest

---

55   The scholia identify the author of this proposal (also mentioned by two other comic poets) as Archinus, a moderate politician who would play a role in the restoration of the democracy in 403.

56   Speaking to the Chorus.

57   Athena.

worthily of your festival
and be garlanded in victory.
Hey now,
let your song invite the youthful god as well,   395
our travel companion in this dance.

(*strophe*)

Exalted Iacchus, inventor of most enjoyable
festive song, come and march along with us
to the goddess,   400
and show us how effortlessly
you get through a long trek.[58]
Iacchus lover of choruses, escort me on my way.

(*antistrophe a*)

For it was you who, for a joke
and for economizing, had my sandals split   405
and my rags tattered,[59]
and you who found a way for us
to frolic and dance without charge.
Iacchus lover of choruses, escort me on my way.

(*antistrophe b*)

Just now in fact I stole a glance
at a young girl, a very pretty one too,   410
a playmate,
and where her dress was torn I saw
her titty peeking out.
Iacchus lover of choruses, escort me on my way.

Dionysus

I've always been an eager
follower, and want to play with her
as I dance.

Xanthias

    Me too!   415

---

58   From Athens to Eleusis, about twelve miles.

59   The chorus, in character as initiates, wear the customary old clothing but also
     call attention to the producer's cheapness in providing their costumes—no
     doubt a result of the Athenians' financial straits at this time. According to the
     scholiast, citing Aristotle (fragment 630), two producers were assigned to each
     competitor at the City Dionysia this year, because not enough candidates could
     be found who could afford to undertake the expense alone.

Chorus

> So what say we get together
> and ridicule Archedemus?[60]
> At seven he still hadn't cut his kinsdom teeth,[61]
> but now he's a leading politico
> among the stiffs above,   420
> and holds the local record for rascality.
> And I hear that Cleisthenes' son
> is in the graveyard, plucking
> his behind and tearing his cheeks;[62]
> all bent over, he kept beating his head,   425
> wailing and weeping
> for Humpus of Wankton, whoever that may be.[63]
> And Callias, we're told,
> that son of Hippocoitus,[64]
> fights at sea in a lionskin made of pussy.[65]   430

Dionysus

> Now could you please tell us
> where hereabouts Pluto dwells?
> We're strangers who've just arrived.

Chorus

> You haven't very far to go
> and needn't question me again: 435
> I'll have you know you're right at his door.

---

60   The prosecutor of one of the commanders at Arginusae, known as "Bleary Eyes" and mocked elsewhere for foreign ancestry.

61   Punning on *phrateras* ("brethren" of a phratry, a kinship association) and *phrasteres* (permanent teeth). Enrollment of a boy in his father's phratry normally took place in his first year, and was considered proof of legitimate birth and citizen status.

62   No son of Cleisthenes is otherwise attested; alternative possibilities are "Cleisthenes' asshole is...plucking and tearing its cheeks," or (with a variant reading) "Cleisthenes is...plucking...his asshole and tearing his cheeks." Graveyards were venues for prostututes.

63   "Sebinus of Anaphlystus" (suggesting *se binein* "fuck you" and *anaphlan* "masturbate") is evidently a fictitious name; it recurs in *Assemblywomen*.

64   Callias (*c.* 450-*c.* 366), ridiculed in comedy for extravagance and debauchery since the 420s, by the 390s had largely squandered the fortune left him by his father Hipponicus whose name is here distorted for a pun on *kinein* "screw."

65   Or "dressed in a lionskin fights a pussy at sea." Pussy translates the obscene Greek term for female genitalia.

Dionysus

Hoist it up again, boy.

Xanthias

This whole routine is nothing
but "Zeus' Cootie-rinthus" in the bedclothes.[66]

Chorus

Go forward now   440
to the goddess' sacred circle, and in her blossoming grove
frolic, you who partake in the festival dear to the gods.
I will go with the girls and the women,
to carry the sacred flame where they revel all night for the
        goddess.

(*strophe*)

Let us go forward to the flowery
meadows full of roses,
frolicking in our own style   450
of beautiful dance,
which the blessed
Fates array.

(*antistrophe*)

For us alone is there sun
and sacred daylight,   455
for we are initiated,
and righteous was our behavior
towards strangers
and ordinary people.

SCENE III: PLUTO'S PALACE (460-673)

*(Dionysus, Xanthias, Aeacus, Maid, Chorus,
Innkeeper, Plathane, Maids and Slaves)*

Dionysus

So how should I be knocking at the door?   460
Hmm. I wonder how the locals hereabouts knock?

Xanthias

Stop dillydallying. Just tuck into that door;

---

66   "Zeus' son Corinthus" (here with a pun on *koreis* "bedbugs") meant "the same
      old story."

show you've got Heracles' guts as well as his garb.

Dionysus
Boy! Boy!

Aeacus[67]
Who's that?

Dionysus
The mighty Heracles.

Aeacus
You loathesome, shameless, insolent piece of scum you!   465
Utter scum! Scum of the earth! And scummiest!
You're the one who rustled our dog Cerberus,
grabbed him by the throat, darted off, and got clean away,
the dog I was in charge of! Ah but now you're in a hammerlock,
such is the black-hearted rock of Styx, and such   470
the blood-dripping crag of Acheron that hem
you in, and the coursing hounds of Cocytus,
and the hundred-headed Echidna, who shall lacerate
your vitals, while the Tartessian moray clutches
your lungs, and Teithrasian Gorgons[68] tear your bleeding   475
balls, and your intestines along with them!
Whom I on rapid foot shall now go fetch.

Xanthias
Hey, what's the matter?

Dionysus
My butt runneth over; let us pray.

Xanthias
Stand up right now, you clown, before somebody   480
sees you that we don't know!

Dionysus
But I feel faint.
Please, give me a wet sponge for my heart.

---

67   The son of Zeus and Aegina and father of Peleus, who with Minos and
     Rhadymanthus judged souls in Hades, but also popularly thought of, much
     like St. Peter later, as Pluto's gatekeeper and steward. In Critias' play *Perithous*
     (fragment 1) he had similarly accosted and questioned Heracles on his way to
     rescue Theseus and Perithous from the underworld.

68   Teithras was an Attic deme, presumably inhabited by formidable ladies, unless
     the epithet is merely an anticlimactic jingle with "Tartessian" in the previous
     line.

Xanthias
> Here, apply this. Where are you putting it? Ye golden gods,
> is that where you keep your heart?

Dionysus
>   Yes, it got scared
> and sneaked down to my colon. 485

Xanthias
> You're the very worst coward in heaven and earth!

Dionysus
>   Who me,
> a coward? Me, who asked you for a sponge,
> something no other man would have dared?

Xanthias
>   What else?

Dionysus
> If he were a coward, he'd have lain in his own stink.
> But I got up, and wiped myself as well. 490

Xanthias
> Poseidon, what bravery!

Dionysus
>   That's certainly what I think.
> Say, weren't you terrified by those noisy rants
> and threats?

Xanthias
>   Nope, never even gave them a thought.

Dionysus
> Very well, then, if you're such a brave he-man,
> you can take this club here and impersonate me, 495
> and take the lionskin too, if you're such a hard-ass.
> As for me, I'll take my turn being your bellboy.

Xanthias
> Then hand them right over; after all, an order's an order.
> Now take a look at Xanthio-Heracles,
> and see if I turn into a yellow-belly like you. 500

Dionysus
> Not a chance: you're that whip-fodder from Melite

to the life![69] Now let me hoist this baggage here.

Enter MAID from the palace.

Maid

Heracles, sweetheart, is that you? Come right on inside.
When the goddess heard you'd come, she started baking
bread, heating two or three pots of split-pea soup,   505
barbecuing a whole ox, and putting pies
in the oven, dinner rolls too.[70] Now come on in!

Xanthias

Thanks, you're too kind.

Maid

              I absolutely won't
stand by and watch you leave! Listen, she was stewing
some bird-meat too, and she was toasting munchies,   510
and she was mixing up some very sweet wine.
Now come on in with me!

Xanthias

               I'm quite fine.

Maid

                     Nonsense,
I'll not let you get away. Listen, there's a girl
piper in there already, very pretty,
and two or three dancing girls too.

Xanthias

              Say again? Dancing girls?   515

Maid

Yes, in first flower and freshly depilated.
Now come in, because the cook was just about
to take the fish off the grill, and the table's set.

Xanthias

Then go on ahead, and tell those dancing girls
that I'll be coming right along, in person.   520

Exit MAID into the palace.

---

69   Heracles had a temple in the deme (political district) of Melite, but the scholia
see here an allusion to Callias, earlier mentioned as wearing a lionskin and
referred to also by the comic poet Cratinus as a whipped slave (fragment 81).

70   It was not customary for the mistress of a household to do cooking herself (least
of all cooking meat) instead of slaves or a professional cook (as in line 517).

Boy, come along here, and bring our luggage in.
Dionysus
Hold on, you're not really taking it seriously,
my having some fun by dressing you up as Heracles?
Now stop your kidding around, my Xanthias,
pick up that baggage and start carrying it again.   525
Xanthias
What? You're not really thinking about taking back
what you gave me, are you?
Dionysus
                        Not maybe, I'm doing it!
Off with that lionskin.
Xanthias
                        Witnesses take note!
I'm putting this in the gods' hands.
Dionysus
                        Gods indeed!
And how brainless and vain of you, a mortal slave,   530
to think that you could be Alcmene's son![71]
Xanthias
Oh all right, then, take them. But there may come a time
when you'll be needing me again, god willing.
Chorus
(*strophe*)
      The mark of a man
      with brains and sense,
      one who's voyaged far and wide,   535
      is ever to shift
      to the comfy side of the ship
      and not just stand fast
      in one position, like a painted
      picture; to roll over
      to the softer side
      is the mark of a smart man,   540
      a born Theramenes.[72]

71 I.e. Heracles, son of Zeus and Alcmene.
72 A leading politician nicknamed "Buskin" (a boot that fits either foot) for his knack
    of landing on his feet in any situation: in 411 he had helped both to establish
    and to overthrow the Four Hundred, and after Arginusae he had transferred
    onto his colleagues the blame for failing to rescue Athenian shipwrecks.

Dionysus
(antistrophe)
Wouldn't it be hilarious
if Xanthias, a mere slave,
were lying all atumble
on Milesian coverlets, and kissing
a dancing girl, then asked for a potty,
and I was looking over at him
with my weenie in hand,   545
and he too caught me watching,
recognizing a fellow rascal, then
punched me in the mouth and knocked out
my front row of chorus men?

Enter from the side a female INNKEEPER with her Maid.

Innkeeper
Plathane![73] Plathane, come here! Here's that hooligan,
the one who came to the inn that time and gobbled   530
down sixteen loaves of our bread!

Enter PLATHANE with her Maid.

Plathane
                                          Oh my god,
he's the very same one!

Xanthias
                                    Somebody's in for it.

Innkeeper
And on top of that, twenty half-obol orders of stew
at one go!

Xanthias
               Somebody's gonna pay for that.

Innkeeper
And all that garlic!

Dionysus
                                 Nonsense, my good woman,   555
and ignorant of the facts.

---

73   The name (derived from *plathanon*, kneading board) was not uncommon but
     appropriate for this character.

Innkeeper
                    Hah! You didn't think
I'd recognize you again if you wore those buskins.
Well? I haven't even mentioned all that fish!

Plathane
Right, dearie, or all those fresh cheeses either
that he ate up along with the baskets they came in!   560

Innkeeper
And then, when I presented him with the bill,
he gave me a nasty look and started bellowing.

Xanthias
That's his style exactly; he acts that way everywhere.

Innkeeper
And he drew his sword like a lunatic.

Plathane
Amen, my poor dear.

Innkeeper
                    We were so terrified   565
that somehow we jumped right up into the loft,
while he up and dashed away with our mattresses.

Xanthias
That's also just his style.

Innkeeper
                    Well, we should do something
about it! Go tell my patron, Cleon, to come here.[74]

Plathane
And you fetch mine, Hyperbolus,[75] if you see him,   570
so we can get the fellow good.

Innkeeper
                    You filthy hog,
Oh how I'd love to take a rock and bash
your teeth out, since they gobbled all my goods!

---

74 Speaking to her maid. Cleon was the leading politician of the 420s, a champion
    of ordinary citizens, and notorious for his zeal as a prosecutor, especially of the
    wealthy; he had died in 422.

75 Speaking to her maid. Hyperbolus was Cleon's successor, and also much satirized
    in comedy; he had died in 411.

Plathane
> And me, I'd love to toss you into the death pit![76]

Innkeeper
> And I'd love to get a sickle and cut out   575
> your gizzard, that guzzled all my sausages!
> Now I'm off to fetch Cleon; he'll summons this guy today
> and wind the very stuffing out of him!

> *Exit INNKEEPER and PLATHANE*

Dionysus
> May I miserably die if I don't love Xanthias!

Xanthias
> I know what you're thinking, I know. Stop talking, stop.   580
> I'll not be Heracles again.

Dionysus
>   Don't say that,
> my little Xanthikins.

Xanthias
>   Sure, how could I,
> a mere mortal slave, become Alcmene's son?

Dionysus
> I know you're angry, and you've every right to be.
> You could even punch at me and I wouldn't say a word.   585
> But I swear: if I take it away from you again,
> may I die a sorry death and be eradicated,
> and my wife and kids, and bleary Archedemus![77]

Xanthias
> I accept your oath, and will take the gear on those terms.

Chorus
> (*strophe*)
> > Now it's up to you,   590
> > since you've accepted the outfit
> > you wore before, to revive anew
> > your old fighting spirit,
> > and once more look formidable,

---

76   The Barathron, a pit situated just outside Athens along the wall leading to Piraeus, where certain convicts were thrown to their death.

77   See line 417.

mindful of the god
whose guise you're taking on.
If you're caught jabbering,
if you utter anything wimpish,   595
you'll be forced to hoist
the baggage once again.

Xanthias

(*antistrophe*)
Gentlemen,[78] that's not bad advice,
but just now I happened to be
thinking along those lines myself.
Yes, I'm quite aware
that if anything good's to be gained
he'll try to take this outfit back.   600
But all the same you'll find me
brave in spirit,
with a pungent look in my eye.
And I'd better be, because I hear,
yes, a clattering at the door.

AEACUS bursts out of the door, with two Slaves.

Aeacus

Tie up this dog thief here and make it quick,   605
so he can be punished. Quickly!

Dionysus

                                        Somebody's in for it!

Xanthias

Stay the hell away, you two!

Aeacus

                                Oh, it's a fight you want?
Hey Ditylas! Hey Sceblyas! Hey Pardocas,[79]
come on outside and fight that guy over there.

Enter from the house Ditylas, Sceblyas, and Pardocas;
they attack and subdue Xanthias.

---

78 The conventional way to address to a mixed audience (the Chorus included women, i.e. chorusmen impersonating women, cf. 323 ff.).

79 Names of (or suggesting) Scythian archers, who were state slaves used in Athens as police.

Dionysus

Shocking, isn't it, the way this guy steals from people   610
and then assaults them too!

Aeacus

Quite monstrous.

Dionysus

Terrible even, and shocking!

Xanthias

Now look here, dammit,
I hope to die if I've ever been here before,
or ever stole so much as a hair of your property!
And I'll make you quite a gentlemanly offer: 615
take my slave here and torture him, and if you catch me
in any wrongdoing, then take me and put me to death.[80]

Aeacus

And how should I torture him?

Xanthias

Any way you like.
Bind him to the ladder. Hang him up. Bristle-whip him.
Flay him. Rack him. Pour vinegar up his nose.   620
Put bricks on him. Anything at all, except
don't beat him with a stalk of leek or onion.

Aeacus

Fair enough. And of course if my beating maims your slave,
the compensation will be credited to your account.

Xanthias

Never mind that; just drag him off and torture him.   625

Aeacus

No, I'll do it here, so that he can testify
to your face. You, drop that baggage quick, and see
that you tell no lies here.

Dionysus

Somebody's hereby warned

---

80 Slaves could not be witnesses in Athenian courts unless their testimony was
obtained under duress and with the consent of the owner, the conditions being
agreed between the owner and his adversary. In practice, offers by an owner
or challenges by an adversary were only very infrequently accepted. Under
Athenian law, citizens could not be tortured.

not to torture me, because I'm immortal. Otherwise,
you'll have only yourself to blame.

Aeacus

What are you talking about? 630

Dionysus

I'm saying that I'm immortal, Dionysus
son of Zeus, and he's the slave.

Aeacus

You hear that?

Xanthias

Yes I do.

And all the more reason he be flogged:
if he really is a god, then he won't feel it.

Dionysus

All right, since you claim that you're a god as well, 635
shouldn't you be getting the very same beating as me?

Xanthias

That's fair enough. And whichever of us you catch
yelping first, or caring at all that he's getting
flogged, that one you can consider to be no god.

Aeacus

You are beyond question a gentleman, the way 640
you take the high road. Now both of you two strip.

Xanthias

So how are you going to test us fairly?

Aeacus

Simple:

stroke for stroke in turn.

Xanthias

That's fine with me.
OK, now see if you catch me flinching. Well,
have you hit me yet?

Aeacus

Zeus no.

Xanthias

That's what I thought. 645

Aeacus

All right, now I'll hit this other one.

Dionysus

Say when.

Aeacus

But I just hit you!

Dionysus

Then why didn't I sneeze?

Aeacus

No idea. I'll try this other one again.

Xanthias

Then hurry up! Ow! Ow!

Aeacus

Why the "ow" "ow", eh?

Did that hurt?

Xanthias

Hell no, I was just thinking   650

when the Heracles festival at Diomeia is scheduled.

Aeacus

The man's sanctified. Let's go back the other way.

Dionysus

Hi yo!

Aeacus

What's the matter?

Dionysus

I see horsemen.

Aeacus

So why are you crying?

Dionysus

I can smell the onions![81]

Aeacus

Meaning you didn't feel anything?

Dionysus

Couldn't care less!   655

---

81 Typical cavalry rations.

Aeacus
Then I'd better go back over to this other one.

Xanthias
Ahh!

Aeacus
What's the matter?

Xanthias
Do take out this thorn.

Aeacus
What's going on here? Got to go back over here.

Dionysus
Apollo! —who abide on Delos or in Pytho.

Xanthias
That hurt him, didn't you hear?

Dionysus
No it didn't!   660
I was just recollecting a line of Hipponax.[82]

Xanthias
Look, you're getting nowhere: just bash him in the ribs.

Aeacus
God no: instead, stick out your belly now.

Dionysus
Poseidon!

Xanthias
Somebody felt that!

Dionysus
—who hold sway   665
on the cape of Aegae or in
the depths of the deep blue sea.[83]

Aeacus
By Demeter, I for one can't make out which
of you is a god. But go along inside;
the master himself will be able to recognize you,   670
and Pherrephatta,[84] because they're both gods too.

---

82   The renowned sixth-century iambic poet from Ephesus; but this verse is ascribed
by a scholiast to Hipponax's contemporary, Ananius.

83   From Sophocles' play, *Laocoon* (fragment 371).

84   Persephone's Attic name.

Dionysus

That's correct. But this is what I wish: that you
had thought of that before I took the beating!

Exit AEACUS, DIONYSUS, XANTHIAS, and Slaves into the palace.

PARABASIS OF THE CHORUS (674-737)

(Chorus)

Chorus

(strophe)

Embark, Muse, on the sacred dance,
and come to inspire joy in my song,   675
beholding the great multitude of people,
where thousands of wits are in session
more high-reaching than Cleophon,[85]
on whose bilingual lips   680
some Thracian swallow
roars terribly,
perched on an alien petal,
and bellows the nightingale's weepy
song, that he's done for,
even if the jury's hung.[86]   685

Chorus Leader

It's right for the sacred chorus to join in giving good advice
and instruction to the city. First then, we think that all
the citizens should be made equal, and their fears removed.[87]
And if anyone was tripped up by Phrynichus' holds,[88] I say
that those who slipped up at that time should be permitted   690
to dispose of their liability and put right their earlier mistakes.
Next I say that no one in the city should be disenfranchised,

---

85 The most influential popular politician in the period after the restoration of
    democracy in 410, and executed in 404 (after the second performance of *Frogs*:
    cf. 1504) on trumped-up charges brought by anti-democratic forces; he was the
    titular character in the play by Platon that competed against the first *Frogs*.

86 Cleophon's father was Athenian, but his mother was portrayed in Platon's play
    and other comedies as a Thracian.

87 I.e., fears of prosecution or attack for offenses they had committed under the
    oligarchy of 411, in spite of the amnesty of 410.

88 One of the leaders of the Four Hundred, whose assassination in summer 411
    accelerated the fall of their regime.

for it's a disgrace that veterans of a single sea battle should
    forthwith
become Plataeans, turning from slaves into masters;[89]
not that I have any criticism to voice about that—   695
indeed I applaud it as being your only intelligent action—
but it's also fitting, in the case of people[90] who fought many a sea
    battle
at your side, and their fathers too, and who are your blood
    relations,
that you pardon this one misadventure when they ask you to.
Now relax your anger, you people who are naturally most sage,
and let's readily accept as kinsmen and as citizens   701
in good standing everyone who fights aboard our ships.
If we puff ourselves up about this and are too proud to do it,
especially now that we have a city "embraced by high seas,"[91]
there will come a time when we'll seem to have acted
    thoughtlessly.   705

Chorus

    (*antistrophe*)
        "If I read aright the life or character
        of a man"[92] who's sure to be sorry yet,
        then this monkey who's so annoying now—
        pint-sized Cleigenes,[93]
        the basest bathman of all   710
        the ash-mixers who lord it over
        fake washing soda
        and fuller's earth—
        he won't be around much longer, and knows it,
        so he's unpeaceable, for fear that some night   715
        on a drunken stroll without his stick
        he'll be mugged.

---

89   Refugees of the Spartan massacre at Plataea in 427 were given Athenian citizen-
      ship (Thucydides 3.68, Demosthenes 59.104-6), just as had the slaves who rowed
      in the battle of Arginusae.

90   I.e., those disenfranchised in 411.

91   Archilochus, fragment 213.

92   Adapted from a tragedy by Ion of Chios.

93   The only Cleigenes attested at this time served as Council Secretary in 410/9
      and is perhaps the predatory litigator of Lysias 25.25 (though the manuscripts
      of that speech read "Cleisthenes").

Chorus Leader

It has often struck us that the city behaves the same
toward those of its citizens who are fine and upstanding
as it does with respect to the old coinage and the new gold.[94] 720
Though both of these coinages are unalloyed, indeed
are considered the finest of all coins, the only coinages
that are minted true and tested everywhere
among the Greeks and among the barbarians alike,
we don't use them;[95] instead we use these crummy coppers, 725
struck yesterday or the day before with a stamp of the lowest
  quality.[96]
Just so with our citizens: the ones we acknowledge to be
well-born, well-behaved, just, fine, and outstanding men,
men brought up in wrestling schools, choruses, and the arts,
we treat them shabbily, while for all purposes we choose the
  coppers, 730
the aliens, the redheads,[97] bad people with bad ancestors,
the latest arrivals, whom formerly the city wouldn't readily
have used even as scapegoats. But even at this late hour,
you fools, do change your ways and once again choose the good
  people.
You'll be congratulated for it if you're successful, 735
and if you take a fall, at least the intelligent will say
if something does happen to you, you're hanged from a worthy
  tree.

---

94 The "old" was the traditional coinage made of silver from the Laureium mines, largely incapacitated since the enemy occupation of Deceleia, and the "new," issued in 407/6, was made from the dedications to Victory on the Acropolis.

95 Because they were earmarked for external payments, e.g. for imports and mercenaries.

96 Silver-plated bronze coins issued along with the new gold coins; they were removed from circulation at some time between 403 and 392.

97 Conventional of Thracians (cf. 681), and in later comedy of slaves.

SCENE IV: SLAVE TALK (738-829)

(*Slave of Pluto, Xanthias, Chorus*)
Enter from the palace XANTHIAS and a SLAVE of Pluto.

Slave
I swear by Zeus the Savior, that master of yours
is a gentleman.

Xanthias
                        Of course he's a gentleman:
a guy who only knows about boozing and balling.   740

Slave
But not to have beaten you as soon as you,
the slave, were caught pretending to be the master!

Xanthias
Then he'd have regretted it!

Slave
                                    Well, you certainly talk
like a true slave! I like talking that way myself.

Xanthias
You like it? I'm interested.

Slave
                                    Why, it's like nirvana   745
whenever I curse my master behind his back!

Xanthias
Ande what about muttering when you leave the house
after getting a heavy beating?

Slave
                                    I love that too.

Xanthias
And what about meddling?

Slave
                                    Positively nonpareil!

Xanthias
Ah Zeus of True Kin! And eavesdropping on masters   750
when they're gossiping?

Slave
                                    I'm simply mad about it!

Xanthias

And what about blabbing it to outsiders?

Slave

Who, me?
Why, doing that gives me an actual orgasm!

Xanthias

By Phoebus Apollo, give me your right hand,
and let's exchange kisses. Now tell me something, by Zeus,   755
our mutual god of floggings, what's all this
commotion inside the palace, all this yelling
and name-calling?

Slave

It's Aeschylus and Euripides.

Xanthias

Aha.

Slave

An event's underway, a big event
among the dead, and intense factionalism.   760

Xanthias

What about?

Slave

There's a traditional custom down in these parts:
in each of the most important and skilled professions,
the one who's best of all his fellow professionals
is entitled to maintenance in the Prytaneum
and a seat next to Pluto[98]—

Xanthias

I get the picture.

Slave

—till someone arrives who is more competent
in the same craft, which means he must step down.

Xanthias

So why would that have flustered Aeschylus?

---

98   At Athens, free meals in the Prytaneum (the official building housing the sacred
hearth) and privileged seating at public events were awarded for outstanding
athletic, military, or political achievement.

Slave
> It was he who held the Chair of Tragedy,
> for being the one most dominant in that art.   770

Xanthias
> Who holds it now?

Slave
>   When Euripides came down,
> he began recitals[99] for the muggers and purse
> snatchers and the father-beaters and burglars
> (there's a lot of them in Hades), and when they heard
> his disputations and his twists and dodges,   775
> they went crazy for him and considered him the best,
> and that inspired him to claim the chair
> that Aeschylus occupied.

Xanthias
>   And wasn't he pelted?

Slave
> He was not; the public clamored to hold a trial
> to determine just who's better in that art.   780

Xanthias
> The criminal public clamored?

Slave
>   Yes, to high heaven.

Xanthias
> But weren't there others who sided with Aeschylus?

Slave
> The good are the minority, just like up here.[100]

Xanthias
> So what does Pluto intend to do about it?

Slave
> To hold a contest immediately, a test   785
> and trial of the artistry of both.

Xanthias
>   And how come
> Sophocles didn't stake a claim to the chair?

---

99   Such as sophists would deliver in order to advertise their intellectual or rhetorical skills.
100 Indicating the spectators.

Slave

Not him! When *he* came down here, Aeschylus
gave him a kiss and took hold of his hand,
and he withdrew any rival claim on the chair.[101]   790
And now he's ready, in the words of Clidemides,[102]
to take a bye and sit it out. If Aeschylus wins,
he'll stay where he is; but otherwise, he promises
to challenge Euripides for the sake of his art.

Xanthias

So it's going to happen?

Slave

Yes, and pretty soon.   795
And then we'll see impressive events set in motion.
Poetic art will be weighed up in a balance—

Xanthias

They'll be weighing tragedy like Apaturia cutlets?[103]

Slave

—and they'll be bringing out rulers, and measuring tapes
for words, and folding frames—   800

Xanthias

So they'll be making bricks?

Slave

—and set squares and wedges; because Euripides says
he's going to examine the tragedies word for word.

Xanthias

I'd guess that Aeschylus is pretty sore about that.

Slave

Well, he did put his head down and glowered like a bull.

Xanthias

And who's to be the judge?

Slave

That was a tough one,   805
because both discovered a shortage of competent people.

---

101 Or, with the mss., "when he came..he kissed Aeschylus and grasped his hand,
and *he* [in contrast with Euripides] withdrew..."

102 Unknown.

103 A kinship festival to which fathers brought sacrificial meat to celebrate their
sons' coming of age; an element of the ritual was the weighing of the meat.

You see, Aeschylus wouldn't agree to use Athenians—

Xanthias

Maybe he considered too many of them crooks.

Slave

—and the rest of them he thought were absolute piffle
when it comes to judging what poets really are.   810
Then they turned it over to your master, since
he's familiar with the art. But let's go inside now:
serious business for masters means affliction for us.

> *XANTHIAS and SLAVE go inside; various
> measuring instruments are brought onstage.*[104]

Chorus

Surely fearful wrath will fill the heart of the mighty
     thunderer
when he sees the sharp-talking tusk of his rival in art   815
being whetted; then with fearful fury
will his eyes whirl about.
We'll have helmet-glinting struggles of tall-crested words,
we'll have linchpin-shavings and chisel-parings of artworks
as a man fends off a thought-building hero's   820
galloping utterances.
Bristling the shaggy-necked shock of his hirsute ridge of
     mane,
his formidable brow frowning, with a roar he will hurl
utterances bolted together, tearing off timbers
with his gigantic blast.   825
Then the smooth tongue unfurling, mouth-working
tester of words, slipping the reins of envy
will sort out those utterances and parse clean away
much labor of lungs.

---

104 These will not be used until much later in the contest (lines 1364 ff.) but
     are brought onstage now in order to pique the spectators' curiosity in the
     meantime.

CONTEST: PRELIMINARIES (830-870)

(Euripides, Dionysus, Aeschylus)

Three chairs are brought out; then enter PLUTO, who takes the center chair, and DIONYSUS (now normally costumed), who takes the left-hand chair; then enter AESCHYLUS, who takes the right-hand chair, followed by EURIPIDES, who lays hands on it; alternatively, the whole tableau may be rolled out on the eccyclema.

Euripides

Give me no lectures, I won't let go the chair!   830
I say I'm better at the art than he is.

Dionysus

Why so quiet, Aeschylus? You hear his claim.

Euripides

He'll be haughtily aloof at first, the same way
he tried to mystify us in his tragedies.

Dionysus

Careful, my friend, don't speak too confidently!   835

Euripides

I know this fellow, and long have had him pegged:
he's a creator of savages, a boorish loudmouth,
with an unbridled, unruly, ungated mouth,
uncircumlocutory, a big bombastolocutor.

Aeschylus

Is that so, you scion of the greenery goddess?[105]   840
This about me from you? You babble-collector,
you creator of beggars,[106] you stitcher of old rags!
Oh, you'll be sorry you said it!

Dionysus

                              Stop it, Aeschylus:
heat not your innards to a state of wrathful rage.[107]

---

105 Adapted from Euripides' phrase "you scion of the sea goddess" (fragment 885). The origin of Aristophanes' allusions to Euripides' mother, who in fact was of high birth, as a hawker of wild herbs (first in *Acharnians*, produced twenty years earlier) is obscure.

106 Most memorably in his *Telephus*, produced in 438, and in earlier comedies Aristophanes mentions several other examples.

107 Probably quoting or adapting an Aeschylean line.

Aeschylus

> No, not till I've manifestly shown him up,   845
> this creator of cripples, for all his impudence.

Dionysus

> A lamb, my boys, bring out a black lamb here!
> For there's a hurricane fixing to hurtle our way!

Aeschylus

> Oh you collector of Cretan arias,[108]
> who brought unholy couplings into our art—   850

Dionysus

> Hold on there, my exalted Aeschylus!
> And you, rascally Euripides, if you have
> any sense you'll move out of the way of this hailstorm,
> or in his anger he may bash your skull
> with a crushing comeback and dash out your *Telephus*.[109]   855
> And you, Aeschylus, give and take arguments
> not angrily but calmly; it's unseemly
> for upstanding poets to squabble like bread women,
> but you start right in roaring like an oak tree on fire.

Euripides

> I'm ready if he is—and I won't back out—   860
> to go first in an exchange of peckings at my words,
> my songs, the sinews of my tragedies,
> including, yes, my *Peleus* and my *Aeolus*,
> my *Meleager*, and even my *Telephus*.

Dionysus

> And what do you want to do, Aeschylus? Do say.   865

Aeschylus

> I would have preferred not to do any wrangling here,
> since the contest isn't on equal terms.

Dionysus

> > How so?

---

108   Referring perhaps to the songs' setting (cf. lines 1356-60), choreographic accompaniment, or mythical content, e.g. Pasiphae and Phaedra.

109   Aristophanes had extensively parodied *Telephus* in *Acharnians* and *Women at the Thesmophoria*.

Aeschylus

> Because my poetry hasn't died with me,
> while his is as dead as he is, so he'll have it
> here to recite.[110] But if that's your decision, so be it.   870

CONTEST: OPENING RITUALS (871-894)

(Dionysus, Chorus, Aeschylus, Euripides)

Dionysus

> Then someone bring me incense and fire here,
> and I'll preface the intellectualisms with a prayer
> that I may judge this contest with the utmost artistic
> integrity. Meanwhile, invoke the Muses in song.

The Chorus performs while Dionysus lights incense and silently prays.

Chorus

> Zeus' nine maiden daughters immaculate,   875
> o Muses, who oversee the keen and subtly reasoning minds
> of men who mint ideas, when they come into conflict,
> debating each other with knotty and precisely plotted ploys,
> come and behold the power
> of two mouths most formidable at purveying   880
> hewn chunks and whittlings of words.
> Yes, now the great intellectual contest
> at last goes into action.

Dionysus

> Now each of pray before you say your piece.   885

Aeschylus

> Demeter, who nurtured my intelligence,
> may I be worthy of your Mysteries!

Dionysus

> You put incense on the fire too.

Euripides

>   No thanks;
> the gods I pray to are a different set of gods.

---

110 Sometime after Aeschylus' death and before 425, a decree was enacted permitting Aeschylus' plays (uniquely) to be entered in competition against new plays, and at least by the time of Plato's *Republic* (2.383c), written in the 370s, Aeschylus' plays were being read in schools.

Dionysus
Some private gods, a novel coinage?

Euripides
Precisely.[111]   890

Dionysus
Then go ahead, pray to these unofficial gods.

Euripides
Sky, my nourisher, and Pivot of Tongue,
and Smarts, and Nostrils keen to sniff things out,
may I correctly refute any arguments I grab!

CONTEST: GENERAL ISSUES (895-1098)

(Chorus, Chorus Leader, Euripides, Dionysus, Aeschylus)

Chorus
(strophe)

And now we're eager   895
to hear from two smart men
a real ballet of words.
Embark on the warpath!
Their tongues have gone wild,
their spirit lacks no boldness,
nor are their minds unmoved.
So it makes sense to expect   900
that this one will say something sophisticated
and finely honed,
while that one will launch his attack
with arguments torn up by the roots,
and scatter great dustclouds of words.

Chorus Leader
Now you must start speaking at once, and be sure to come out
with   905
sophisticated material, not riddles or stuff just anyone could say.
Euripides
Very well, as for myself, the kind of poet I am,
I'll reveal in my final remarks; but first I'll expose my opponent

---

111 A charge commonly brought against intellectuals, most notably Socrates in
399.

for the charlatan and quack that he was, and how he
    hoodwinked
his audiences, whom he took over from Phrynichus[112] already
    raised   910
to be morons. He'd always start by having some solitary
    character
sit muffled up, say Achilles or Niobe, not letting us see their face
(a poor excuse for tragic drama!) or hear even *this* much of a
    peep.

Dionysus

That's true, he didn't.

Euripides

And while they sat there in silence, his chorus would rattle off
four suites of choral lyric one after another without a break.   915

Dionysus

I enjoyed those silences, and found them no less pleasant
than the chatterboxes we get nowadays.

Euripides

                                    Well, that's because
you were naive.

Dionysus

                    I think so too. But what was the fellow up to?

Euripides

Pure charlatanism, so the spectator would sit there waiting for
    the moment
when his Niobe would make a sound; meanwhile the play went
    on and on.   920

Dionysus

What a devil! The way I was taken in by him!
Why are you fussing and fidgeting?[113]

Euripides

                              Because I'm exposing him.
And then, when he'd humbugged along like that and the play
    was half over,
he'd come out with a dozen words as big as an ox

---

112 A tragic poet who was an older contemporary of Aeschylus.
113 To Aeschylus.

with crests and beetling brows, formidable bogey-faced
>things 925
unfamiliar to the spectators.

Aeschylus

>Good grief!

Dionysus

>>Be quiet!

Euripides

And he wouldn't say one intelligible word—

Dionysus

>>Stop gnashing your teeth![114]

Euripides

—but only Scamanders, or moats, or shields bronze-bossed and
>blazoned
with griffin-eagles, and huge craggy utterances
that were't easy to decipher.

Dionysus

>>By heaven, I myself 930
"have lain awake through long stretches of night trying
to figure out"[115] the kind of bird a tawny horsecock is.

Aeschylus

It was carved on the ships[116] as a figurehead, you ignoramus!

Dionysus

And here I thought it was Philoxenus' son, Eryxis![117]

Euripides

But really, should one write about a *rooster* in tragedy? 935

Aeschylus

And you, you enemy of the gods, what subjects did you write
>about?

Euripides

Certainly not about horsecocks or goatstags, like you,
the sort of things they embroider on Persian tapestries.

---

114 To Aeschylus.

115 Adapted from Euripides, *Hippolytus* 375-76.

116 I.e. the ships at Troy.

117 Probably Eryxis of Cephisia, who had recently had a seat on the Council and
(to infer from this context) a naval command.

No, as soon as I first inherited the art from you,
bloated with bombast and obese vocabulary,   940
I immediately put it on a diet and took off the weight
with a regimen of wordlets and strolls and little white beets,
administering chatter-juice pressed out of books;
then I built up its strength with an admixture of Cephisophon's
    arias.[118]
And I didn't write whatever humbug entered my head, or
    charge in   945
and make a mess, but the very first character who walked on
    stage began
by explaining the play's origins.

Aeschylus
                        Because they were lots better than your own!

Euripides
    Again, from the very first lines I wouldn't leave any character
        idle;
    I'd have the wife speak, and the slave just as much, and the
        master,
    and the maiden, and the old lady.
    Aeschylus
    And for such audacity   950
    you surely deserved the death penalty!

Euripides
                        No, by Apollo:
    it was a democratic act.[119]

Dionysus
                        Better change the subject, my friend;
    that's hardly the very best theme for a sermon from *you!*[120]

Euripides
    Then I taught these spectators how to talk—

---

118 Cephisophon was evidently a close friend of Euripides; the later tradition that
    he helped write Euripides' plays and seduced his wife was probably derived
    from comedy, though Euripides' marital difficulties seem real enough: see below,
    lines 1046-48.

119 That women and slaves should have any kind of equality with adult male citizens
    was in fact a radical idea.

120 Shortly before his death, Euripides had emigrated to Macedonia at the invitation
    of King Archelaus.

Aeschylus

I'll say you did!
If only you'd split in two before you had the chance!   955

Euripides

—and how to apply subtle rules and square off their words,
to think, to see, to understand, to be quick on their feet, to
    scheme,
to see the bad in others, to think of all aspects of everything—

Aeschylus

I'll say!

Euripides

—by staging everyday scenes, things we're used to, things that
    we live with,
that I wouldn't have got away with falsifying, because these
    spectators   960
knew them as well as I and could have exposed my faulty art.
I never distracted their minds with bombastic bluster, never
    tried
to shock them by creating Cycnuses and Memnons with bells on
    their horses'
cheek plates.[121] You can judge by comparing his followers and
    mine:
his are Phormisius[122] and Megaenetus the Stooge,[123]   965
bugle boys with long beards and lances, flesh-ripping pine-
    benders,
while mine are Clitophon[124] and the sharp Theramenes.[125]

Dionysus

Theramanes? That man's formidably intelligent across the board:
if he happens to get into trouble or even comes close to it,

---

121   Trojan allies slain by Achilles; Memnon was a character in *Memnon* and *Weighing of Souls*, but Cycnus cannot be assigned to any Aeschylean play on present evidence.

122   A moderate democrat whose beard suggested female genitalia.

123   Otherwise unknown.

124   A supporter and then an enemy of the Four Hundred; Plato portrays him as an associate of the sophist Thrasymachus.

125   See line 541 n.

he gives that trouble the slip, not a bust after all but a
    blackjack![126]   970

Euripides

That's how I encouraged
these people to think,
by putting rationality into my art,
and critical thinking,
so that now they grasp and really understand   975
everything, especially how to run their households
better than they used to, and how to keep
an eye on things: "How's this going?"
"Where'd that get to?" "Who took that?"

Dionysus

Heavens yes, these days each   980
and every Athenian comes home
and starts yelling at the slaves,
demanding to know "Where's the pot?
Who chewed the head off
this sprat? The bowl I bought   985
last year is shot!
Where's that garlic from yesterday?
Who's been nibbling olives?"
They used to sit there like dummies,
gaping boobies,   990
Simple Simons.

Chorus

(*antistrophe*)

    "You behold all this, glorious Achilles!"[127]
    But what will you say in reply?
    Only take care
    that your anger doesn't seize you
    and drive you off the track,   995
    for his accusations are formidable.
    Yes, take care, good sir,
    that you don't reply in a rage,
    but shorten your sails   1000

---

126 Lit. "not a Chian [the lowest throw at dice] but a Cean [punning on 'Coan,' the highest throw, and suggesting foreign ancestry or a connection with the Cean philosopher Prodicus]."

127 The opening line of Aeschylus' *Myrmidons* (fragment 131).

and cruise with them furled,
then little by little make headway
and keep watch for the moment
when you get a soft, smooth breeze.

Chorus Leader

Now then, you who were the first of the Greeks to rear towers of
majestic utterance
and adorn tragic rant, take heart and open the floodgates! 1005

Aeschylus

I'm enraged at this turn of events, and it sours my stomach
that I have to debate this man, but I don't want him claiming I'm
at a loss,
so answer me this: for what qualities should a poet be admired?

Euripides

Skill and good counsel, and because we turn people into better
members of their communities.

Aeschylus

And if you haven't done this, 1010
but rather turned good, upstanding people into obvious
scoundrels,
what punishment would you say you deserve?

Dionysus

Death; you needn't ask *him*!

Aeschylus

Then just consider what they were like when he took them over
from me,
noble six-footers and not the civic shirkers,
vulgarians, imps, and criminals they are now, 1015
but men with an aura of spears, lances, white-crested helmets,
green berets, greaves, and seven-ply oxhide hearts.

Dionysus

This goes from bad to worse: making helmets now—he'll wear
me out!

Euripides

And just how did you train them to be so noble?

Dionysus

Speak up, Aeschylus, and don't be willfully prideful and
difficult. 1020

Aeschylus
By composing a play chock-full of Ares.

Dionysus
Namely?

Aeschylus
My *Seven Against Thebes;*
every single man who watched it was hot to be warlike.

Dionysus
Well, that was an evil accomplishment, because you've made the
Thebans[128]
more valiant in battle, and you deserve a beating for it.

Aeschylus
No, you could all have had the same training, but you didn't
take that path.   1025
Thereafter I produced my *Persians,* which taught them to yearn
always to defeat the enemy, and thus I adorned an excellent
achievement.[129]

Dionysus
I certainly enjoyed it when they listened to the dead Darius,
and the chorus clapped their hands together like this and cried
"aiee!"   1029

Aeschylus
That's the sort of thing that poets should practice. Just consider
how beneficial the noble poets have been from the earliest times.
Orpheus revealed mystic rites to us, and taught us to abstain
from killings;
Musaeus gave us oracles and cures for diseases; Hesiod
agriculture,
the seasons for crops, and ploughing; and where did the godlike
Homer
get respect and renown if not by giving good instruction   1035
in the tactics, virtues, and weaponry of men?

---

128 The Thebans were bitter enemies of Athens in the Peloponnesian War.
129 The defeat of the Persians at Salamis (in 480) and Plataea (479).

Dionysus

Yes, but all the same
he didn't succeed with that lummox Pantacles,[130] who just the
other day,
in a parade, was trying to fasten the crest to his helmet after he'd
put it on!

Aeschylus

But surely he did succeed with many other brave men, one of
whom
was the hero Lamachus;[131] from that mold my imagination
created   1040
many profiles in courage, men like Patroclus and the lionhearted
Teucer,
in hopes of inspiring every citizen to measure himself against
them
whenever he heard the bugle. But I certainly created no whores
like Phaedra and Stheneboea,[132] and no one can find a lustful
woman in anything I ever composed.

Euripides

No, because Aphrodite had nothing to do with you.

Aeschylus

And may she never!   1045
Whereas she plunked herself down plenty hard on you and
yours,
and yes, even flattened you personally.

Dionysus

That's the truth, all right!
You yourself got hit by the same stuff you wrote about other
people's wives.[133]

---

130 Ridiculed in the same terms by the comic poet Eupolis in the 420s (fragment
318).

131 His distinguished military career began in the 430s and ended with a coura-
geous death in action in 414 (Thucydides 6.101); though Aristophanes portrayed
him as a braggart soldier in *Acharnians*, he praised him after his death (*Women
at the Thesmophoria* 841).

132 Both heroines (of Euripides' *Hippolytus* and *Stheneboea* respectively) proposi-
tioned a stepson (Hippolytus, Bellerophon) and then accused him of rape when
rejected.

133 Since no awareness of a marital scandal involving Euripides appears in *Women
at the Thesmophoria* (Dionysia 411), it must have occurred later, and there may be
an allusion to it in fragment 596, which probably comes from *Gerytades* (produced
in 408).

Euripides

> And what harm did my Stheneboeas do to the community, you
> bastard?

Aeschylus

> You motivated respectable women, the spouses of respectable
> men,   1050
> to take hemlock in their shame over your Bellerophons.

Euripides

> But the story I told about Phaedra was already established,
> wasn't it?

Aeschylus

> Of course it was. But the poet has a special duty to conceal
> what's wicked,
> not stage it or teach it. For children it is the teacher who
> instructs,
> but grownups have the poet. It's very important that we tell
> them   1055
> things that are good.

Euripides

> So if you give us stuff like Lycabettus and massy
> Parnassus,[134] that's supposed to teach what's good? You should
> have done
> your instructing in plain human language.

Aeschylus

> Look, you wretch, great thoughts
> and ideas force us to produce expressions that are equal to them.
> And anyway, it suits the demigods to use exalted
> expressions,   1060
> just as they wear much more impressive clothing than we do;
> that's where I set a good example that you completely corrupted

Euripides

> How so?

Aeschylus

> First, you made your royals wear rags, so that
> they'd strike people as being piteous.

---

134 Mountains.

Euripides

So what harm did I do there?

Aeschylus

Well, for one thing, that's why no rich man is willing to
command a warship,   1065
but instead wraps himself in rags and whines, claiming to be
poor.[135]

Dionysus

When, by Demeter, he's actually wearing a soft woollen shirt
underneath!
And if he pulls off that lie, he pops up in the fish market![136]

Aeschylus

Then you taught people to cultivate chitchat and gab,
which has emptied the wrestling schools and worn down the
butts   1070
of the young men as they gab away, and prompted the the crew
of the *Paralus*
to talk back to their officers.[137] Yet in the old days, when I was
alive,
all they knew how to do was shout for their rations and cry
"heave ho!"

Dionysus

God yes, and fart in the bottom bencher's face,
and smear shit on their messmates, and steal people's clothes on
shore leave!   1075
Now they talk back and refuse to row, and the ship sails this
way and that.

Aeschylus

And what evils can't be laid at his door?
Didn't he show women procuring,[138]
and having babies in temples,[139]   1080

---

135 A trierarchy was a service levied on the rich, who could sue for exemption by
demonstrating insufficient wealth to a jury.

136 Seafood was relatively expensive.

137 One of two triremes used for state business, whose all-citizen crew were strongly
democratic.

138 Phaedra's nurse in *Hippolytus*.

139 The heroine in *Auge*.

and sleeping with their brothers,[140]
and claiming that "life is not life"?[141]
As a result, our community's filled
with assistant secretaries
and clownish monkeys of politicians   1085
forever lying to the people,
and from lack of physical fitness there's nobody left
who can run with a torch.

Dionysus

Amen to that! I about died laughing
at the Panathenaea[142] when some laggard   1090
was running, all pale-faced, stooped over,
and fat, falling behind
and struggling badly; and then at the Gates
of the Potter's Field people whacked
his stomach, ribs, flanks, and butt,   1095
and at their flat-handed slaps
he started farting,
and ran away blowing on his torch!

CONTEST: PROLOGUES (1099-1250)

(Chorus, Euripides, Dionysus, Aeschylus)

Chorus

(*strophe*)

It's a great affair, a great quarrel,
a stern war that's in progress!
So it's a tough task to decide the issue,   1100
when one strives forcefully
and the other can wheel around
and sharply counterattack.
Now don't just sit tight, you two:
there are plenty more thrusts to come,
and more intellectualities.

---

140 Canace with Macareus in *Aeolus*, though this was probably a rape.
141 Perhaps spoken by Pasiphae in *Polyidus*.
142 This annual festival of Athena, among Athens' most splendid events, was
     celebrated with special grandeur every fourth year as the Great Panathenaea,
     most recently the previous summer.

So whatever your grounds of dispute,   1105
argue out, attack, and lay bare
the old and the new,
and take a chance on saying
something subtle and sage.
(*antistrophe*)
And if you're afraid
of any ignorance among
the spectators, that they won't   1110
appreciate your subtleties of argument,
don't worry about that, because
things are no longer that way.
For they're veterans,
and each one has a book
and knows the fine points;
their natural endowments are masterful too,   1115
and now sharpened up.
So have no fear,
but tackle it all, resting assured
that the spectators are sage.

Euripides
Now then, let me turn just to your prologues,
so as first off to examine the first section   1120
of this competent man's tragic drama, because he was
obscure in the exposition of his plots.

Dionysus
And what prologue of his do you mean to examine?

Euripides
                                                A great many.
First off, recite me the one from the *Oresteia*.[143]

Dionysus
Come on, everyone, be quiet! Go ahead, Aeschylus.   1125

Aeschylus
"Underworld Hermes, who watch over the paternal domain,
be now, I pray, my ally and my savior,
for I've come back to this land and now return."

---

143 A tetralogy produced in 458, of which three plays survive (*Agamemnon, Libation Bearers*, and *Eumenides*).

Dionysus
Do you have any criticism of that?

Euripides
                              A dozen or so.

Dionysus
But the whole quotation is only three lines long!   1130

Euripides
And each one of them contains about twenty mistakes.

Dionysus
Aeschylus, I advise you to keep quiet, or else
you'll be shown liable for even more than three iambics!

Aeschylus
Me keep quiet for him?

Dionysus
                              If you take my advice.

Euripides
I say he's made a mistake of cosmic scale.   1135

Aeschylus
Listen to you rant!

Dionysus
                    Go on; it matters little to me.

Aeschylus
What mistake do you refer to?

Euripides
                              Recite it again.

Aeschylus
"Underworld Hermes, who watch over the paternal domain."

Euripides
Now doesn't Orestes say this at the tomb
of his dead father?

Aeschylus
                    That's exactly right.   1140

Euripides
So let me get this right: after his father had died
violently at his wife's hands in a secret plot,
he was saying that Hermes "watched" while this was
    happening?

Aeschylus
> He certainly was not! He called on Nether Hermes
> as "Underworld Hermes" and made it clear that Hermes   1145
> possesses this function as a paternal inheritance.

Euripides
> That's an even bigger mistake than I was looking for!
> Because if he has the underworld as a paternal inheritance—

Dionysus
> That would make him a graverobber on his father's side!

Aeschylus
> Dionysus, the wine you're drinking has gone sour.   1150

Dionysus
> Recite him another one, and you watch for the mistake.

Aeschylus
> "Be now, I pray, my ally and savior,
> for I've come back to this land and now return."

Euripides
> Sage Aeschylus has told us the same thing twice.

Dionysus
> How twice?

Euripides
> Examine the expression, and I'll show you.   1155
> "I've come back to this land," he says, "and now return;"
> but "coming back to" is the very same as "returning."

Dionysus
> Of course! It's like asking your neighbor, "Lend me
> a kneading trough, or else a trough to knead in."

Aeschylus
> That's not the same thing at all, you fool   1160
> for folderol! The wording is excellent.

Dionysus
> How so? Explain to me what you mean by that.

Aeschylus
> Anyone who belongs to a country can "come back" to it;
> he just arrives with no further circumstance.
> But an exile both "comes back" and "now returns."   1165

Dionysus
Very good, by Apollo! What do you say, Euripides?

Euripides
I deny that Orestes was coming home; he arrived
secretly and without informing the authorities.

Dionysus
Very good, by Hermes, though I don't know what you mean.

Euripides
Well, let's have another line.

Dionysus
Yes, go right ahead,   1170
Aeschylus; and you keep an eye out for the mistake.

Aeschylus
"And at this burial mound I invoke my father,
to hearken and hear—"

Euripides
There again the same thing twice:
"hearkening" and "hearing" are quite obviously identical.

Dionysus
Yes, but he was addressing the dead, you chump,   1175
and we can't reach them even if we speak three times!
But how did you compose *your* prologues?

Euripides
I'll tell you.
And if anywhere I say the same thing twice,
or you spot irrelevant padding, just spit on me.

Dionysus
Go ahead, recite one. I'm more than eager to hear   1180
the verbal precision of your own prologues.

Euripides
"At first was Oedipus a lucky man,—"

Aeschylus
He certainly was not; he was born unfortunate,
seeing that he's the one who, even before his birth,
Apollo said would kill his father—before   1185
his very conception! So how "at first a lucky man"?

Euripides
"—but then he became the wretchedest of mortals."

Aeschylus

No, certainly not "became," for he never stopped!
Considering that as a newborn they put him in
a pot and exposed him in the dead of winter,   1190
so that, grown, he wouldn't become his father's murderer;
then he wandered off on two swollen feet to Polybus;
then while still a young man he married an old lady;
and on top of that she was his very own mother;
then he blinded himself.

Dionysus

                              Yes, he was a lucky man,   1195
if he also shared command with Erasinides![144]

Euripides

That's hogwash. I compose prologues very well.

Aeschylus

Look here, I certainly don't intend to pick away
at your expressions word by word; instead, gods willing,
I'll demolish those prologues of yours with an oil bottle.[145]   1200

Euripides

My prologues with an oil bottle?

Aeschylus

                              With only one.
You compose so that anything can be tagged right on
to your iambics, "tuft of wool," "oil bottle,"
or "little sack." And I'll show you how right now.

Euripides

You'll show me, eh?

Aeschylus

                    I will.

Euripides

                              So I'd better recite one.   1205
"Aegyptus, as the story is most widely disseminated,

---

144 Among the admirals at the battle of Arginusae who were put to death for failing
   to rescue the shipwrecked sailors.

145 *Lekythion*, the small round flask (today referred to as aryballos) in which a man
   might carry oil for use at the gymnasium or baths.

by sailor's oar together with his fifty sons,
made for Argos and—"[146]

Aeschylus

Lost his oil bottle.

Dionysus

What's with this oil bottle? To hell with it!
Recite him another prologue, so I can hear that again.

Euripides

"Dionysus, decked out with wands and fawnskins midst
the pines, from the slopes of Mount Parnassus, leaps
in the dance and—"[147]

Aeschylus

Lost his oil bottle.

Dionysus

Oh my, we're struck once more by that oil bottle!

Euripides

Well, this is no big deal. Here is a prologue   1210
he can't attach an oil bottle to:
"No man exists who's blessed in every way;
he may have been noble born yet lacking livelihood,
or may have been low born and—"[148]

Aeschylus

Lost his oil bottle.

Dionysus

Euripides?

Euripides

What?

Dionysus

I think you should reef your sails;   1220
that oil bottle's blowing up a gale.

---

146 From *Archelaus*, according to the scholia, but ancient scholars could not locate
these lines in the version available to them; presumably the opening in their
text had been revised, either by Euripides or (more likely, since this was among
Euripides' last plays) by later performers.

147 From *Hypsipyle* (fragment 752).

148 From *Stheneboea* (fragment 661).

Euripides

    Quite the contrary, I'm worried not at all.
    For this time it'll be knocked right out of his hand.

Dionysus

    Then recite another, and dodge that oil bottle.

Euripides

    "Cadmus, Agenor's son, departed Sidon's   1225
    citadel, and—"[149]

Aeschylus

              Lost his oil bottle.

Dionysus

    My loopy friend, do buy that oil bottle,
    so he won't be mangling our prologues.

Euripides

                       What's that you say?
    Me buy from him?

Dionysus

              If you listen to my advice.

Euripides

    I won't, because I can recite a lot of prologues   1230
    where he won't be able to attach an oil bottle.
    "Pelops, the son of Tantalus, came to Pisa
    on swift steeds and—"[150]

Aeschylus

              Lost his oil bottle.

Dionysus

    There, he attached that oil bottle again!
    My man, there's still time: please make him an offer.   1235
    You'll get it for an obol, and it's fine quality.

Euripides

    No indeed, not yet; I've still got heaps of prologues.
    "Once Oeneus from his land—"[151]

---

149 From the second *Phrixus* (fragment 819).

150 From *Iphigeneia among the Taurians* (lines 1-2).

151 From *Meleager*, but not the opening lines (fragment 515), which do not allow the tag!

Aeschylus

Lost his oil bottle.

Euripides

You might at least let me finish the whole line first!
"Once Oeneus from his land reaped a bounteous harvest,   1240
and while sacrificing first fruits—"

Aeschylus

Lost his oil bottle.

Dionysus

In the middle of his sacrifice? And who swiped it?

Euripides

Never mind, good sir; let him respond to this:
"Zeus, as the true version of the story goes—"[152]

Dionysus

You'll be the death of me,[153] because he's going to say   1245
"lost his oil bottle."[154] Yes, that oil bottle
grows on your prologues like sties on eyes. So for heaven's
sake, please turn to his choral lyrics now.

Euripides

In fact, I've got the evidence to prove
he's a bad lyricist and recycles the same old thing.   1250

CONTEST: LYRICS (1251-1363)

(Chorus, Euripides, Dionysus, Aeschylus)

Chorus[155]

(1) How will this affair proceed?
I simply can't imagine
what criticism he aims to make
of a man who composed
more lyrics of the finest quality   1255

---

152 From *Wise Melanippe*, of which the first 22 lines survive (fragment 481).

153 Or with a possible alternative reading, "he'll be the death of you..."

154 For whatever reason, Aristophanes has Euripides end with a prologue where
this would *not* have been possible.

155 (1) 1252-56 and (2) 1257-60 are apparently authorial variants, probably composed
for the first (2) and the revised (1) versions of the play; (2) has perhaps lost one
or more lines at the end.

than anyone else to this day.
(2) I simply can't help wondering
how he aims to criticize
this Bacchic lord,
and I'm afraid for him.   1260

Euripides

So many wonderful lyrics, eh? We'll soon find out,
for I'll trim all his lyrics down to a single pattern.

Dionysus

Very well, and I'll pick up some pebbles to count them off.

Euripides

Phthian Achilles, why, when you hear the slaughter of
    heroes,—
Aiee the strike!—draw you not near to the rescue?[156]   1265
We, the people of the lake shore, honor Hermes our
    forebear—[157]
Aiee the strike!—draw you not near to the rescue?

Dionysus

That's two strikes against you, Aeschylus.

Euripides

Most reknowned of Achaeans, puissant child of Atreus,
    hearken to me when I say—[158]   1270
Aiee the strike!—draw you not near to the rescue?

Dionysus

That's strike three, Aeschylus!

Euripides

Keep holy silence! The Bee Governesses are nigh
to open the temple of Artemis—[159]
Aiee the strike!—draw you not near to the rescue?   1275
I've mastery yet to declare the propitious drive of wayfaring
    heroes.[160]
Aiee the strike!—draw you not near to the rescue?

---

156 From *Myrmidons* (fragment 132).
157 From *Ghost Raisers* (fragment 273).
158 Ancient scholars could not identify the source.
159 From *Priestesses* (fragment 87).
160 *Agamemnon* (line 104).

Dionysus

    Lord Zeus above, that was quite a volley of strikes!
    I think I'd better get to the bathhouse now,
    because these strikes have made my kidneys sore!   1280

Euripides

    No, wait till you've also heard the second set
    of choral lyrics, made from tunes for the lyre.

Dionysus

    Go ahead with it then, but please include no strikes.

Euripides

    How the twin-throned command of the Achaeans,
    the flower of Greece—   1285
        brumda brumda brumda brum
    sends the Sphinx, Head Bitch of Bad Days—
        brumda brumda brumda brum
    with avenging spear and arm, did the warlike bird of
        omen—
        brumda brumda brumda brum
    that gave her into the hands of the nasty hounds   1290
    that roam the sky—
        brumda brumda brumda brum
    and the company clinging to Ajax—
        brumda brumda brumda brum.[161]   1295

Dionysus

    What's this brumda brumda brumda brum? Where did
    you collect these rope-winders' songs? from Marathon?

Aeschylus

    No matter, because I took them from a good source
    for a good purpose: so I wouldn't be caught culling
    the same sacred meadow of the Muses as Phrynichus,   1300
    whereas this one takes material from everywhere:
    whore ditties, drinking songs by Meletus,[162]
    pipe tunes from Caria, dirges, and dance music.
    Someone hand me my lyre! Then again, who needs
    a lyre for this job? Where's that female percussionist   1305

---

161 Based on *Agamemnon*, lines108-11, with phrases inserted from *Sphinx* (fragment 236), *Thracian Women* (fragment 84), and perhaps *Memnon* (cf. the scholia on 1291-92).

162 A sixth- or possibly early 5th-century erotic poet.

who plays on potsherds? Hey, Muse of Euripides,
come here; you're the proper accompanist for these songs.

Enter Muse of Euripides.

Dionysus
This Muse never gave throat to a Lesbian tune![163]

Aeschylus
You halcyons, who chatter by the everflowing
waves of the sea,   1310
wetting and bedewing the skin
of your wings with rainy drops;
and you spiders in crannies beneath the roof
who with your fingers wi-i-i-i-nd
loom-taut spoolings,   1315
a recital by the minstrel loom,
where the pipe-loving dolphin leaped
at the prows with their dark rams
for oracles and race tracks.
Sparkle of the vine's winey blossom,   1320
anodyne tendril of the grape cluster,
throw your arms around me, child![164]
Notice that foot?

Euripides
    I do.

Aeschylus
And this one, see that?

Euripides
    I do.

Aeschylus
And you who compose such stuff   1325
have the nerve to criticize my songs,
you who turn out lays à la Cyrene's
Twelve Tricks?[165]

---

163 A reference to the Lesbian musical tradition (e.g. Sappho) and to fellatio (associated by the Athenians with Lesbos), and implying both musical and sexual unattractiveness (since fellatio was a specialty of older whores).

164 A pastiche from *Hypsipyle*, with snippets from *Meleager* and *Electra* (lines 435-37).

165 Cyrene was famous courtesan.

That will do for your choral lyrics; now I want
to take a close look at the meter of your arias.   1330

> O darkness of Night gloomily gleaming,
> what baleful dream do you send me,
> an emanation from obscure Hades,
> a thing of lifeless life,
> ghastly child of black Night,   1335
> a fearful sight,
> shrouded in cadaverous black,
> with murderous murderous stare
> and big claws?
> Now handmaidens, light me a lamp,
> fetch river dew in buckets,
> and heat the water,
> that I may wash away the god-sent dream.   1340
> Oho god of the deep,
> it's come to pass! Oho my fellow lodgers,
> behold these marvels: my rooster
> Glyce has snatched, and vanished!
> Nymphs of the mountains,
> and you, Mania,[166] help me!   1345
> I, poor thing,
> happened to be seeing to my own
> chores, wi-i-i-inding in my hands
> a full spindle of flax
> as I made my cloth, so I could get   1350
> to the market before sunup
> and sell it.
> But he flew up flew up to the sky
> on the lightest of wingtips,
> leaving to me but woes woes,   1355
> and tears tears from my eyes
> did I shed in my misery.
> Now you Cretans, children of Ida,
> snatch up your bows and assist me!
> Shake a leg aleap
> and surround her house!

---

166 A typical name for a slave or freedwoman.

And with you let the fair maid Dictynna[167]
take her pack of bitches and run
all throughout her halls.   1360
And you, Hecate, daughter of Zeus,
brandishing in your hands the most searing
flame of your twin torches,
light my way to Glyce's,
so I can go in and search!

CONTEST: WEIGHING OF VERSES (1364-1410)

(Dionysus, Aeschylus, Euripides)

Dionysus
Now both of you stop the songs.

Aeschylus
                                          I've had enough too;
what I'd like to do is take him to the scales,[168]   1365
which is the only true test of our poetry;
the weight of our utterances will be the decisive proof.

Dionysus
Come over here then, if that's what I really must do,
weighing the art of poets as if I were selling cheese.

Chorus
Experts are indefatigable,   1370
for here is another marvel,
startling and altogether eccentric;
who else could have thought it up?
Gee, even if some chance passerby
had told me about this,   1375
I wouldn't have believed him,
I'd have thought he was drivelling.

Dionysus
Now both of you stand by the scale pans.

---

167 A Cretan goddess similar to Artemis.

168 The following weighing scene was probably modelled on the scene in Aeschylus'
lost play *Weighing of Souls*, where Zeus weighed the souls of Achilles and
Memnon as they fought a duel.

Aeschylus and Euripides

Here we are!

Dionysus
Now each take hold of your pan and speak a line,
and don't let go till I give a cuckoo call. 1380

Aeschylus and Euripides
Ready!

Dionysus
Now each speak your line right into the scales.

Euripides
"Would that the good ship *Argo* ne'er had winged her way."[169]

Aeschylus
"O river Spercheius and the haunts where oxen graze."[170]

Dionysus
Cuckoo!

Aeschylus and Euripides
There they go!

Dionysus
Look, this one's going down
much lower!

Euripides
And just why did it do that? 1385

Dionysus
Why? He put in a river, wetting down
his line as a wool merchant wets his wool,
while you put in a line with wings upon it.

Euripides
Let him speak another and weigh it against mine.

Dionysus
Then take hold again.

Aeschylus and Euripides
We're ready!

Dionysus
Speak away! 1390

---

169 *Medea* (line 1).
170 From *Philoctetes* (fragment 249).

Euripides
"Persuasion's only temple is the spoken word."[171]

Aeschylus
"For the only god who covets no gifts is Death."[172]

Dionysus
Let 'em go!

Aeschylus and Euripides
They're off!

Dionysus
His went down farther again,
because he put in Death, the heaviest blow.

Euripides
But I had Persuasion, a word that's always fitting.   1395

Dionysus
Persuasion's a lightweight without a mind of its own.
Try to find something else this time, something heavyweight,
big and strong enough to depress your pan.

Euripides
Hmm, where have I got something like that? Hmm.

Dionysus
I suggest
"Achilles's cast is two ones and a four."[173]   1400
Each speak your lines, and this is your final weighing.

Euripides
"He took in hand the handle heavy with iron."[174]

Aeschylus
"Chariot upon chariot, and corpse upon corpse."[175]

Dionysus
He's got the better of you once again!

Euripides
How so?

---

171 From *Antigone* (fragment 170).
172 From *Niobe* (fragment 161).
173 A poor throw in dice; the line either comes from a play of Euripides unknown
to ancient scholars or was invented by Aristophanes.
174 From *Meleager* (fragment 531).
175 From *Glaucus of Potniae* (fragment 38).

Dionysus

> He put two chariots and two corpses in: 1405
> not even a hundred Egyptians could lift all that!

Aeschylus

> No more of this line-by-line for me; he could
> get in that pan himself, with his wife, his kids,
> and Cephisophon, and take his books along too,
> and I'd only have to recite two of my lines.   1410

CONTEST: POLITICS (1411-1466)

(Pluto, Dionysus, Aeschylus, Euripides)

Dionysus

> These men are my friends, and I'll not judge between them;
> I don't want to get on the bad side of either of them.
> For one I consider a master, the other I enjoy!

Pluto

> Then you won't accomplish your mission here at all.

Dionysus

> And what if I do reach a verdict?

Pluto

>   The one you choose   1415
> you may take back with you, so you won't have come for
>   nothing.

Dionysus

> God bless you! Now listen to me, you two.
> I came down here for a poet. Why was that?
> So our city, rescued, could continue her choral festivals.
> So whichever of you is prepared to offer the city   1420
> some good advice, he's the one I've decided to take back.

So for starters, which of you has an opinion about
Alcibiades?[176] The city's in travail about him.

Aeschylus
And what does the city think of him?

Dionysus
                                                   I'd say,
it yearns for him, detests him, and wants to have him.[177]   1425
Now both of you tell me what *you* think about him.

Euripides
I detest the citizen who will prove to be slow
to aid his country but quick to do her great harm,
resourceful for himself, incompetent for the city.

Dionysus
Well said, by Poseidon! Now what's *your* opinion?   1430

Aeschylus
(A) It's not good to rear a lion-cub in the city.   1431a
(B) It's best to rear no lion in the city.[178]   1431b
But if you do raise one, then cater to its ways.

Dionysus
By Zeus the Savior, I simply can't decide!
For one spoke sagely, and the other clearly.
So each of you tell me one more good idea   1435
that you have about the salvation of our city.[179]

---

176 This brilliant, aristocratic, and notorious leader was elected to the command
of the Sicilian Expedition in 415 but, soon after it sailed, fled to Sparta to avoid
prosecution in a scandal involving disrepect of the Mysteries; in 411 he broke
with the Spartans and was elected commander by the Athenian fleet, and enjoyed considerable success during the next four years; in 407 he triumphantly
returned to Athens and was elected Supreme Commander, but after the naval
defeat at Notium a few months later was dismissed and retired to an estate on
the Hellespont (Xenophon *Hellenica* 1.5.16-17), where in 404 he was assassinated
on the orders of Lysander. Our passage shows that the issue of his recall was
still a live one in the aftermath of the battle of Arginusae.

177 Adapted from a line in Ion's play, *Guards* (fragment 44).

178 Probably authorial variants, though we cannot tell which belonged to the original
and which to the revision. In Greek poetry, oracular references to the lion often
refer to tyrants or political strongmen.

179 Lines 1437-50 contain authorial variants whose priority and line order are
controversial.

Euripides
>(A) If someone winged Cleocritus[180] with Cinesias,
>and send him on the breeze o'er the watery plain—

Dionysus
>That would be a funny sight! But what's the point?

Euripides
>If there's a naval battle and they carried vinegar   1440
>cruets, they could spray it in the enemy's eyes.   1441

Dionysus
>By Palamedes,[181] that's good; you're a genius!   1452
>Did you think that up yourself, or Cephisophon?

Euripides
>All by myself, but Cephisophon thought up the cruets.

Euripides
>(B) I've got one that I'd like to tell you.

Dionysus
>   Go ahead.   1442

Euripides
>Whenever we put our trust in what's untrusted,   1443
>and what's trustworthy goes untrusted—

Dionysus
>   How's that? I don't follow.   1444
>Try speaking somewhat less cleverly and more clearly.   1445

Euripides
>If we stopped trusting the citizens that we now trust,   1446
>and start making use of the citizens that now   1447
>we don't make use of—

Dionysus
>   Then we'd find salvation?   1448

Euripides
>If we're faring poorly with the current bunch, how wouldn't 1449
>we find salvation if we did the opposite?   1450

---

180 Probably the same Cleocritus who is mentioned in *Birds* (line 877) as a fat man with an ostrich for a mother.

181 The cleverest hero at Troy and a legendary inventor; subject of a play by Euripides that Aristophanes parodied in *Women at the Thesmophoria* (lines 768-84).

Dionysus
And you? What have you got to say?

Aeschylus
Tell me who the city's
making use of now: the good people?

Dionysus
Of course not!   1455
She absolutely hates them.

Aeschylus
But delights in the bad ones?

Dionysus
No, she doesn't; she makes use of them perforce.

Aeschylus
Then how could anyone save a city like that,
if the city won't wear either a cloak or a goatskin?

Dionysus
By god, think of something, if you want to go back up.   1460

Aeschylus
I'll tell you up there, but here I would rather not.

Dionysus
Oh no you don't; send up your blessings from here.

Aeschylus
When they think of the enemy's country as their own,
and their own country as the enemy's; and the fleet
as their wealth; and their wealth as pure despair.   1465

Dionysus
Good, except that the juryman gobbles that all by himself![182]

---

182 Referring to state pay for public services: an emphatic (because gratuitous) anti-democratic sentiment.

CONTEST: VERDICT (1467-1478)

(*Pluto, Dionysus, Euripides, Aeschylus*)

Pluto
Your verdict, please.

Dionysus
                                    This will be my decision between you:
I'll choose the one that my soul wishes to choose.

Euripides
Remembering the gods by whom you swore
that you'd take me back home, now choose your friends.   1470

Dionysus
It was my tongue that swore:[183] I'm choosing Aeschylus.

Euripides
What have you done, you absolute scum of the earth?

Dionysus
Me? I've judged Aeschylus the winner; why shouldn't I?

Euripides
You can face me after acting so disgracefully?

Dionysus
What's disgraceful, if it doesn't seem so to the spectators?[184] 1475

Euripides
You bastard, will you just watch as I stay dead?

Dionysus
Who knows if life isn't really death, and if breath
is merely dinner, and sleep a fleecy blanket?[185]

Exit EURIPIDES.[186]

---

183 Cf. line 101-2, above.

184 From Euripides' *Aeolus* (fragment 19: Macareus defending his incestuous rape
of Canace), with "the spectators" substituted for "those who do it."

185 The first phrase is from Euripides' *Polyidus* (fragment 638).

186 Either he runs off or is wheeled back inside on the *eccyclema*, if it was used (cf.
830 n.).

BON VOYAGE TO AESCHYLUS (1479-1527)

(Pluto, Dionysus, Chorus, Aeschylus)

Pluto
Dionysus, you two go inside now.

Dionysus
                              Why?

Pluto
Let us entertain[187] you before you set sail.[188]

Dionysus
                    Good suggestion,   1480
by Zeus; I certainly can't complain about that!

PLUTO escorts DIONYSUS and AESCHYLUS into the palace.

Chorus
(strophe)
Happy the man who has
keen intelligence,
as is abundantly clear:
this man, for his eminent good sense,   1485
is going back home again,
a boon to his fellow citizens,
a boon as well
to his family and friends,
through being intelligent.   1490
(antistrophe)
So what's stylish is not to sit
beside Socrates and chatter,
casting the arts aside
and ignoring the best
of the tragedian's craft.   1495
To hang around killing time
in pretentious conversation
and hairsplitting twaddle
is the mark of a man who's lost his mind.

---

187 The Greek word (*xenizein*) denotes official hospitality (like our "state dinner") for distinguished guests.

188 As if they were departing from Athens, whose land routes were now cut off.

Enter PLUTO with AESCHYLUS, DIONYSUS, and XANTHIAS.[189]

Pluto

    Fare you well then, Aeschylus,   1500
    and save our city
    with your fine counsels, and educate
    the thoughtless people; there are many of them.
    And take this and give it to Cleophon;[190]
    and this to the Commissioners of Revenue,[191]   1505
    together with Myrmex[192] and Nicomachus;[193]
    and this to Archenomus;[194] and tell them
    to hurry on down here to me,
    without delay; and if they don't
    come quickly, by Apollo   1510
    I'll tattoo them, clap them in leg irons,
    and dispatch them below ground right quick,[195]
    along with Leucolophus' son, Adeimantus![196]

Aeschylus

    That I shall do. And you hand over my chair   1515
    to Sophocles to look after
    and preserve, in case I should
    ever return: for I rank him
    second to me in the art.
    And remember to see to it that that criminal,   1520

---

189 It is likely, though not indicated in the text, that Persephone enters as well, in view of her prominent Eleusinian associations.

190 Cf. 678 n. The objects given by Pluto (and more fittingly carried by Xanthias than by Aeschylus, who will depart carrying a torch) are instruments of suicide, probably a sword, a noose, and a mortar of hemlock (cf. lines 121-34).

191 Nothing is known of their particular functions.

192 Otherwise unknown.

193 Probably the defendant mentioned by Lysias in speech 30 (dated 399/98), who at the time of *Frogs* held an appointment to review, consolidate, and supervise the public inscription of the laws.

194 Otherwise unknown.

195 These punishments were available to masters or overseers with misbehaved slaves.

196 Alcibiades' cousin, who fled Athens after implication in the scandal of the Mysteries in 415, returned in 407, and then served as a general. He was the only Athenian prisoner not executed by the Spartans after the battle of Aegospotami, where he was widely believed to have behaved treasonously, so that the reference here was probably added for the revised production. It may be relevant to Pluto's threat that he had unsuccessfully opposed an Assembly motion to mutilate all enemy prisoners.

that liar, that buffoon,
never sits down on my chair,
not even accidentally.

Pluto

Now you all in this man's honor
display your sacred torches and escort him forth,   1525
hymning his praises
with his own songs and melodies.

EXODUS OF THE CHORUS (1528-1533)

(Chorus)

Chorus

First, you gods below earth, grant to the departing poet
a fine journey as he ascends to the sunlight,
and to the city grant fine ideas that will bring fine blessings.
For that way we may have an end of great griefs   1531
and painful encounters in arms. Let Cleophon do the
     fighting,
and any of those others who wants to fight on his own
     native soil![197]

---

197   Implying non-Athenian ancestry, cf. 678-82, 730-33.